THE AUSTRALIAN
Women's Weekly
delectable
desserts

acp
books

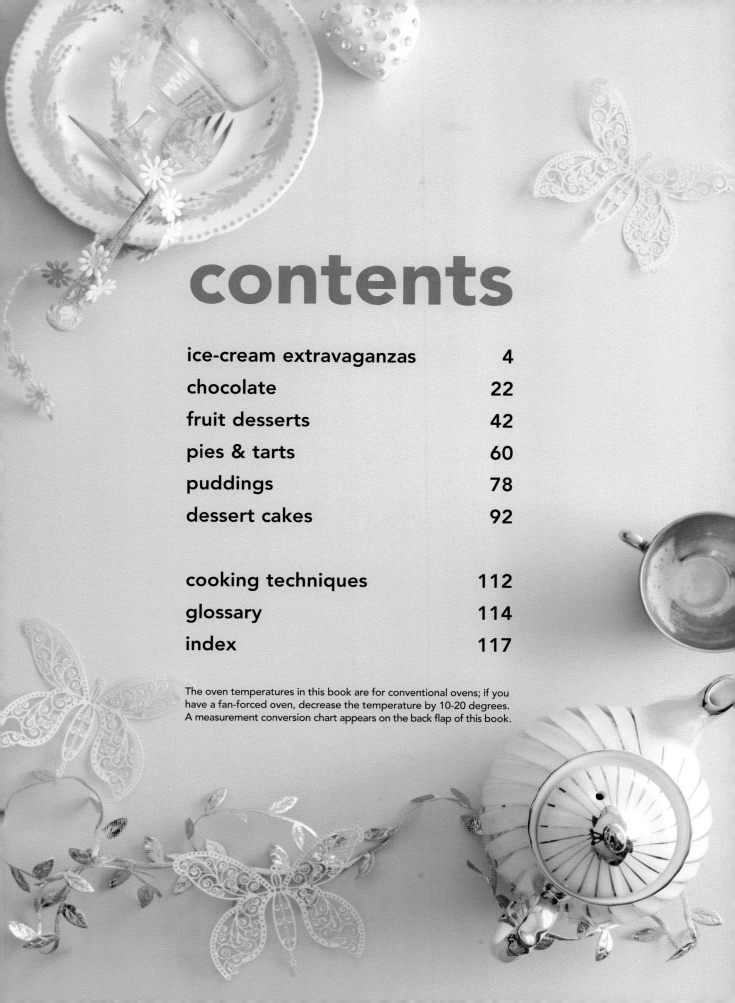

contents

The oven temperatures in this book are for conventional ovens; if you have a fan-forced oven, decrease the temperature by 10-20 degrees. A measurement conversion chart appears on the back flap of this book.

ice-cream extravaganzas

raspberry and passionfruit vacherin

3 egg whites

1 cup (220g) caster (superfine) sugar

6 large passionfruit

3¾ cups (495g) raspberry sorbet

2½ cups (625ml) thickened (heavy) cream (see note)

100g (3 ounces) fresh raspberries

2 teaspoons icing (confectioner's) sugar

1 Have egg whites at room temperature.
2 Preheat oven to 90°C/195°F. Grease two oven trays. Trace 18cm (7¼-inch) circles onto two sheets of baking paper; place paper, traced-side down, on trays.
3 Beat egg whites in small bowl with electric mixer until soft peaks form; gradually add sugar, beating until sugar dissolves. Divide the meringue mixture evenly between marked circles; spread mixture just inside marked lines.
4 Bake meringues about 2 hours or until dry to touch. Cool on trays.

5 Grease 18cm (7¼-inch) (closed) springform pan; line base and side with baking paper.
6 Halve passionfruit; spoon pulp into small measuring jug (you need ½ cup pulp).
7 To assemble vacherin: Beat sorbet a with wooden spoon in medium bowl until softened; stir in passionfruit pulp. Place one meringue, top-side up, in pan; top with sorbet mixture, smooth surface. Freeze about 1 hour or until firm. Top with remaining meringue, top-side down, pressing down gently. Cover with plastic wrap; freeze overnight or until firm.
8 Remove vacherin from pan; place on serving plate. Return to freezer.
9 Beat cream in small bowl with electric mixer until soft peaks form; spread all over vacherin. Top with raspberries. Serve dusted with sifted icing sugar.

prep + cook time 2¾ hours (+ cooling & freezing)
serves 10

note It is fine to use just the one 600ml carton or two 300ml cartons of cream for this recipe.

tips You can vary this dessert endlessly by changing the flavours of the sorbet and the fruit. You can make this dessert ahead of time; once frozen, cover with plastic wrap. Decorate with fresh fruit before serving. If you are not going to eat the entire dessert, cover the cut surfaces with plastic wrap and freeze before it melts.

tropical bombe alaska

You need an ice-cream machine to make the coconut sorbet, or you can buy either coconut sorbet or coconut gelato for this recipe, if you prefer.

1 tablespoon liquid glucose

¾ cup (165g) white (granulated) sugar

1¾ cups (430ml) water

150g (4½ ounces) coconut powder

450g packet rectangular unfilled double sponge cakes (14½ ounces)

2 cups (500ml) mango sorbet

4 egg whites

¾ cup (165g) caster (superfine) sugar

⅔ cup (160ml) water, extra

pinch cream of tartar

rum syrup

¼ cup (55g) caster (superfine) sugar

¼ cup (60ml) water

1½ tablespoons dark underproof rum

1 To make coconut sorbet: Stir glucose, white sugar and ¾ cup of the water in medium saucepan, over medium heat, without boiling, until sugar dissolves. Bring to the boil; boil, uncovered, without stirring, 3 minutes. Cool. Whisk coconut powder and the remaining water in large jug until smooth; stir in glucose mixture. Churn in ice-cream machine following manufacturer's instructions.
2 Using serrated knife, split both cakes in half lengthways. Using a 10-cup (2.5-litre) dolly varden pan or pudding basin as a guide, cut circles from sponge to fit base and top of pan. Grease pan or basin; line with plastic wrap.
3 Line base of pan with sponge. Line side of pan with sponge, cutting sponge to fit. Spoon in mango sorbet; freeze until firm. Top sorbet with a layer of sponge cut to fit, then coconut sorbet; freeze until firm. Top sorbet with remaining sponge, cover pan with plastic wrap; freeze overnight.
4 Make rum syrup.
5 Have egg whites at room temperature.
6 Turn frozen bombe onto serving plate; discard lining. Return to freezer.
7 To make meringue: Stir caster sugar and the extra water in small saucepan, over high heat, without boiling, until sugar dissolves. Bring to the boil, reduce heat, simmer, uncovered, until syrup reaches 115°C/240°F on a candy thermometer. When syrup reaches 115°C, start beating egg whites with cream of tartar in medium bowl with electric mixer until soft peaks form. While beating egg whites, bring sugar syrup to 121°C/250°F. With motor operating, gradually pour hot syrup into egg whites in a thin steady stream; continue beating until mixture is thick, glossy and cooled to room temperature.
8 Working quickly, spread meringue all over sponge. Using a blowtorch, brown meringue until golden. Serve with rum syrup.

RUM SYRUP Stir sugar and the water in small saucepan over high heat, without boiling, until sugar dissolves. Bring to the boil; remove from heat, cool. Stir in rum.

prep + cook time 45 minutes (+ cooling, churning & freezing) **serves** 16

tips When making the meringue, it takes up to 15 minutes for the sugar syrup to reach soft ball stage and then only a few minutes to reach hard ball stage – the syrup must not change colour. As the meringue sets quickly, keep beating it until ready to spread over the bombe. Blowtorches are available from kitchenware and hardware stores. You can serve the bombe alaska without browning it.
You can use bought ice-cream or sorbet such as passionfruit, pineapple or banana instead of the coconut sorbet. You will need to buy 3 cups (750ml).
If you are not going to eat the entire dessert, cover the cut surfaces with plastic wrap and freeze before it melts.

choc-caramel brownie ice-cream sandwich

300g (9½ ounces) dark eating (semi-sweet) chocolate

185g (6 ounces) butter

¼ cup (25g) dutch cocoa powder

1 cup (220g) firmly packed light brown sugar

¾ cup (165g) caster (superfine) sugar

2 teaspoons vanilla extract

4 eggs

1½ cups (225g) plain (all-purpose) flour

2 cups (500ml) caramel swirl ice-cream

chocolate ganache

1¼ cups (310ml) pouring cream (see note)

200g (6½ ounces) dark eating (semi-sweet) chocolate

almond toffee

100g (3 ounces) blanched almonds

1 cup (220g) caster (superfine) sugar

½ cup (125ml) water

1 Preheat oven to 160°C/325°F. Grease two 20cm (8-inch) square cake pans; line with baking paper, extending paper 5cm (2 inches) over sides.

2 Break chocolate into large heatproof bowl; add chopped butter. Place over large saucepan of simmering water; stir until smooth. Remove from heat; whisk in sifted cocoa, sugars and extract until smooth. Stir in eggs and sifted flour.

3 Spread mixture evenly into pans. Bake about 35 minutes; cool brownies in pans. Enclose brownies in plastic wrap, freeze until ready to assemble.

4 Line cleaned 20cm (8-inch) square pan with plastic wrap. Place one brownie, top-side up, in pan.

5 Beat ice-cream in medium bowl a with wooden spoon until barely softened. Working quickly, spread ice-cream over brownie in pan, cover, freeze until firm. Top with remaining brownie, top-side down, press down gently, cover; freeze overnight.

6 Make chocolate ganache and almond toffee.

7 Just before serving, top the brownie sandwich with ganache and broken toffee. Cut into squares to serve.

CHOCOLATE GANACHE Bring cream up to the boil in small saucepan; remove from heat. Break chocolate into cream; stir until smooth. Transfer mixture to small bowl. Refrigerate until firm. Beat ganache with electric mixer until spreadable.

ALMOND TOFFEE Stir nuts in large heavy-based frying pan until golden; remove from pan to baking-paper-lined oven tray to cool. Combine sugar and the water in small saucepan, stir over high heat until sugar is dissolved. Boil, without stirring, for about 10 minutes or until toffee coloured. Remove from heat, allow bubbles to subside. Pour toffee evenly over nuts; leave to set at room temperature.

prep + cook time 45 minutes (+ cooling & freezing) serves 16

note It is fine to use just one 300ml carton of cream for the chocolate ganache.

tips Use a large, sharp hot dry kitchen knife to cut the brownie sandwich into squares. If you are not going to serve it all, it's best to only cut what you need as the cut brownie will dry out in the freezer. Cover the cut surfaces with plastic wrap and freeze before it melts.

triple chocolate sponge surprise

3 eggs

100g (3 ounces) dark eating (semi-sweet) chocolate

2 tablespoons water

¼ cup (55g) caster (superfine) sugar

1 litre (4 cups) dark chocolate ice-cream

350g (11 ounces) milk eating chocolate

1½ cups (375ml) thickened (heavy) cream

200g (6½ ounces) dark eating (semi-sweet) chocolate, extra

⅓ cup (35g) dutch cocoa powder

1 Have eggs at room temperature.

2 Preheat oven to 180°C/350°F. Grease deep 22cm (9-inch) square cake pan; line base and sides with baking paper, extending paper 5cm (2 inches) over sides.

3 Break dark chocolate into small saucepan, add the water; stir over low heat until smooth. Cool to just warm.

4 Separate eggs. Beat egg yolks and sugar in small bowl with electric mixer about 5 minutes or until pale and thick. Beat in chocolate mixture until combined. Transfer mixture to large bowl.

5 Beat egg whites in small bowl with electric mixer until soft peaks form. Fold egg whites into chocolate mixture, in two batches. Pour mixture into pan; smooth surface. Bake about 17 minutes; cool sponge in pan.

6 Place ice-cream in medium bowl; beat a with wooden spoon until barely softened. Spread ice-cream over sponge in pan; smooth surface. Cover with foil; freeze overnight.

7 Break milk chocolate into medium heatproof bowl, place over medium saucepan of simmering water (don't let water touch base of bowl); stir until smooth. Remove from heat; cool to just warm.

8 Meanwhile, beat cream in small bowl with electric mixer until firm peaks form; refrigerate until ready to use. Whisk slightly warm chocolate mixture into cream. Pour over ice-cream layer; smooth surface. Freeze overnight.

9 Finely chop extra dark chocolate; combine with sifted cocoa in medium bowl. Sprinkle chocolate mixture over dessert just before serving.

prep + cook time 1 hour (+ cooling & freezing) serves 12

tips To cut this dessert, use a large hot dry kitchen knife. Cut as many portions as you need, and freeze any remaining dessert covered with foil. Cut the dessert as soon as you take it out of the freezer, but wait about 10 minutes before serving.

jewelled nougat ice-cream with raspberry coulis

1.5 litres (6 cups) nougat ice-cream

200g (6½ ounces) rose-flavoured turkish delight

½ cup (65g) dried cranberries

½ cup (70g) roasted unsalted shelled pistachios

raspberry coulis

300g (9½ ounces) frozen raspberries

½ cup (110g) caster (superfine) sugar

1 tablespoon lemon juice

1 Lightly grease eight 1-cup (250ml) moulds.
2 Place ice-cream in large bowl; stand about 10 minutes or until barely softened.
3 Meanwhile, chop turkish delight coarsely.
4 Stir turkish delight, cranberries and nuts into ice-cream. Spoon and press mixture into moulds, cover with foil; freeze overnight.
5 Make raspberry coulis.
6 Serve ice-cream drizzled with raspberry coulis.

RASPBERRY COULIS Combine ingredients in medium saucepan; cook, covered, over medium-high heat, about 5 minutes or until raspberries are soft. Simmer, uncovered, about 4 minutes or until coulis thickens slightly. Strain coulis through fine sieve into small jug; discard seeds. Cover; refrigerate until ready to serve.

prep + cook time 45 minutes (+ freezing) **serves** 8

tips Use kitchen scissors to cut the turkish delight. Nougat ice-cream is available from some specialist food stores; if you can't find it, use a good-quality vanilla ice-cream instead.

banoffee ice-cream tart with toffeed pecans

170g (5½ ounces) butter

250g (8 ounces) granita biscuits

3 cups (750ml) vanilla ice-cream

½ cup (110g) firmly packed light brown sugar

395g (12½ ounces) canned sweetened condensed milk

⅓ cup (115g) golden syrup or treacle

⅓ cup (80ml) milk

3 small bananas (390g)

1 cup (250ml) thick (double) cream

toffeed pecans

¼ cup (55g) caster (superfine) sugar

2 tablespoons water

5g (¼ ounce) butter

½ cup (60g) pecans

1 Melt 100g (3 ounces) of the butter in small saucepan over low heat. Process biscuits until fine; with motor operating, add the melted butter, process until combined. Press mixture over base and side of 22cm (9-inch) round loose-based fluted flan pan. Place pan on tray; refrigerate 15 minutes.

2 Place ice-cream in large bowl; beat a with wooden spoon until barely softened. Spread ice-cream into tart shell, smooth surface; freeze overnight.

3 Make toffeed pecans.

4 Chop remaining butter, place in medium saucepan with sugar; stir over high heat until smooth. Add condensed milk and golden syrup to pan; bring to the boil. Boil, stirring constantly, about 10 minutes or until sauce is caramel in colour. Remove from heat; stand 10 minutes then gradually stir in milk.

5 Slice bananas thickly. Spread cream over ice-cream; top with banana and toffeed pecans. Serve immediately drizzled with warm caramel sauce.

TOFFEED PECANS Line oven tray with baking paper. Combine sugar and the water in small saucepan; stir over heat, without boiling, until sugar dissolves. Bring to the boil; boil, uncovered, without stirring, until caramel in colour. Remove from heat, allow bubbles to subside; stir in butter and nuts. Pour mixture onto tray; cool. Break toffee into pieces.

prep + cook time 40 minutes (+ refrigeration & freezing) **serves** 10

tip Toffeed pecans can be stored in an airtight container at room temperature for about 4 weeks.

frozen black forest torte

250g (8 ounces) dark eating (semi-sweet) chocolate

125g (4 ounces) butter

⅔ cup (100g) self-raising flour

⅔ cup (150g) caster (superfine) sugar

4 eggs

3 cups (500g) cherry brandy ice-cream

2 cups (500ml) thickened (heavy) cream

¼ cup (40g) pure icing (confectioners') sugar

150g (5 ounces) dark eating (semi-sweet) chocolate, extra

12 fresh cherries (85g)

kirsch syrup

¼ cup (55g) caster (superfine) sugar

¼ cup (60ml) water

2 tablespoons kirsch

red wine and cherry sauce

¾ cup (165g) caster (superfine) sugar

⅔ cup (160ml) water

1⅓ cups (330ml) dry red wine

1 cinnamon stick

3 cloves

200g (6½ ounces) fresh or frozen seeded cherries

1 Preheat oven to 180°C/350°F. Grease two deep 20cm (8-inch) round cake pans; line base and sides with baking paper.

2 Break chocolate into large heatproof bowl over large saucepan of simmering water. Chop butter into bowl; stir until smooth. Cool.

3 Stir sifted flour and caster sugar into chocolate mixture; whisk in eggs until smooth. Pour mixture evenly into pans; bake about 20 minutes. Stand cakes in pans 5 minutes before turning, top-side up, onto wire rack to cool.

4 Meanwhile, make kirsch syrup.

5 Using serrated knife, split each cake in half.

6 When nearly ready to assemble torte, place ice-cream in large bowl; stir with a wooden spoon until barely softened.

7 Using same cleaned cake pan, line with plastic wrap, extending wrap 10cm (4 inches) over side. Place one cake layer in pan; drizzle with 2 tablespoons of the syrup. Top with one-third of the ice-cream. Repeat with remaining cake layers, syrup and ice-cream, finishing with cake; press down firmly. Fold plastic wrap over to enclose; freeze overnight.

8 Make red wine and cherry sauce.

9 Beat cream and sifted icing sugar in small bowl with electric mixer until soft peaks form; refrigerate until ready to use.

10 Remove ice-cream cake from pan; invert onto serving plate, discard lining plastic. Spread cream mixture all over cake. Using a vegetable peeler, make curls from the extra chocolate. Decorate cake with chocolate curls and fresh cherries. Serve with sauce.

KIRSH SYRUP Stir sugar and the water in small saucepan over high heat, without boiling, until sugar dissolves. Bring to the boil. Cool; stir in kirsch.

RED WINE AND CHERRY SAUCE Stir sugar and the water in medium saucepan over high heat, without boiling, until sugar dissolves. Bring to the boil; boil, uncovered, without stirring, about 10 minutes or until caramel in colour. Meanwhile, combine wine and spices in medium saucepan over medium heat. Remove caramel from heat; carefully pour in warm wine mixture. Return to heat; stir until sauce is smooth. Bring to the boil; boil, uncovered, about 8 minutes or until sauce is syrupy and reduced to about ½ cup; discard spices. Add the cherries; stir until heated through. Cool before serving.

prep + cook time 1 hour (+ cooling & freezing) **serves** 12

tips When adding the wine to the caramel, be careful as the mixture will spit and spatter. You can cover the cake with the whipped cream ahead of time and return it to the freezer. Stand at room temperature for about 15 minutes before serving. If you can't get cherry brandy ice-cream you can stir a little cherry brandy through some softened vanilla ice-cream instead; or you can use any ice-cream you like, chocolate or vanilla would work well, too.

vanilla strawberry swirl macaroons

3 egg whites

2½ cups (625ml) vanilla ice-cream

1 cup (120g) ground almonds

1¼ cups (240g) pure icing (confectioners') sugar

¼ cup (55g) caster (superfine) sugar

pink food colouring

strawberry puree

250g (8 ounces) strawberries

2 tablespoons pure icing (confectioners') sugar

1 Have egg whites at room temperature.

2 Make strawberry puree.

3 Grease deep 22cm (9-inch) square cake pan; line base and sides with baking paper, extending paper 5cm (2 inches) over sides.

4 Place ice-cream in medium bowl; beat a with wooden spoon until barely softened. Stir ¼ cup strawberry puree through the ice-cream. Spread into the pan, smooth surface; freeze about 4 hours or until firm.

5 Meanwhile, grease two oven trays; line with baking paper.

6 Process ground almonds and icing sugar until fine; sift through fine sieve into small bowl.

7 Beat egg whites in small bowl with electric mixer until soft peaks form; add caster sugar and a few drops of food colouring, beat until sugar dissolves. Transfer mixture to large bowl; fold in almond mixture.

8 Spoon mixture into piping bag fitted with 2cm (¾-inch) plain tube. Pipe twelve 5cm (2-inch) rounds, about 2cm (¾ inches) apart, onto trays. Tap trays on bench so macaroons spread lightly; stand about 30 minutes or until macaroons feel dry to touch.

9 Meanwhile, preheat oven to 150°C/300°F.

10 Bake macaroons about 20 minutes. Cool on trays.

11 Working quickly, lift ice-cream slab onto board; using 5cm (2-inch) round cutter, cut rounds from ice-cream (they should be the same size as the macaroons). Sandwich macaroons with ice-cream. Serve immediately with remaining puree.

STRAWBERRY PUREE Hull and halve strawberries; blend or process with icing sugar until smooth.

prep + cook time 1 hour (+ freezing, standing & cooling) **makes** 6

tips Serve the macaroons with any leftover ice-cream. Filled or unfilled (baked) macaroons can be frozen in an airtight container for up to three months.
It's important to use pure icing sugar for the macaroons, but it's not necessary for the puree.

vanilla and rhubarb slice

1 bunch rhubarb (500g)

¾ cup (120g) icing (confectioners') sugar

1 tablespoon lemon juice

450g packet rectangular unfilled double sponge cakes (14½ ounces)

1 litre (4 cups) vanilla ice-cream

2 cups (500ml) thickened (heavy) cream

¼ cup (40g) icing (confectioners') sugar, extra

1 cup (80g) flaked almonds

rhubarb compote

½ cup (110g) caster (superfine) sugar

¼ cup (60ml) water

1 Preheat oven to 200°C/400°F. Line oven tray with baking paper.
2 Trim rhubarb; combine with sifted icing sugar and juice in shallow baking dish. Roast, uncovered, about 15 minutes or until rhubarb is tender but still holding its shape; cool on baking-paper-lined tray, reserve juices in dish.
3 Meanwhile, line base and sides of loaf pan with plastic wrap, extending wrap 10cm (4 inches) over sides.
4 Using serrated knife, split one sponge in half lengthways (reserve the remaining sponge for another use), trim and position, cut-side up, in base of pan; freeze 15 minutes. Slightly soften half the ice-cream; spread evenly over sponge in pan. Top ice-cream with about five rhubarb stems, trimmed to fit pan; reserve the remaining rhubarb. Cover pan, freeze about 3 hours or until ice-cream is firm.
5 Slightly soften the remaining ice-cream; top rhubarb with the ice-cream; cover, freeze until firm. Top ice-cream with remaining trimmed sponge, cut-side down. Cover pan; freeze overnight.
6 Make rhubarb compote.
7 Beat cream and extra sifted icing sugar in small bowl with electric mixer until soft peaks form; refrigerate until ready to use.

8 Dry-fry nuts in large frying pan, stirring, over medium heat, until browned lightly; remove from pan, cool.
9 Place cake on serving plate. Spread cake all over with whipped cream; press nuts onto sides. Slice cake, serve with rhubarb compote; accompany with custard or cream, if you like.

RHUBARB COMPOTE Chop reserved rhubarb, place in small saucepan with reserved juices, sugar and the water. Bring to the boil, stirring, until sugar is dissolved. Simmer 2 minutes; cool.

prep + cook time 30 minutes (+ cooling & freezing) **serves** 16

tips Use kitchen scissors to cut roasted rhubarb. You can cover the cake with whipped cream and nuts ahead of time and freeze until ready to serve. The cake will need to stand at room temperature for about 10 minutes to thaw slightly before serving. Make the compote on the day of serving. It can be stored in the fridge; bring to room temperature before serving.

chocolate

hot chocolate soufflés with poached cherries

4 eggs

2 egg whites

2 tablespoons caster (superfine) sugar

200g (6½ ounces) dark eating (semi-sweet) chocolate

¼ cup (55g) caster (superfine) sugar, extra

1 teaspoon icing sugar

3 cups (750ml) vanilla ice-cream

poached cherries

500g (1 pound) fresh cherries

¼ cup (55g) caster (superfine) sugar

5cm (2-inch) strip orange rind

½ cup (125ml) orange juice

½ cup (125ml) water

2 tablespoons orange-flavoured liqueur

1 Make poached cherries.
2 Have eggs and egg whites at room temperature; separate whole eggs.
3 Preheat oven to 200°C/400°F. Grease six ½-cup (125ml) ovenproof (soufflé) dishes with butter, sprinkle butter with caster sugar; shake out excess sugar.
4 Break chocolate into large heatproof bowl over large saucepan of simmering water (don't let water touch base of bowl); stir until chocolate is melted. Cool 5 minutes; stir in egg yolks.
5 Beat all six egg whites and extra sugar in medium bowl with electric mixer until soft peaks form. Fold into chocolate mixture, in two batches. Divide mixture between dishes; smooth tops. Place dishes on oven tray. Bake soufflés about 10 minutes.

6 Dust soufflés with sifted icing sugar. Serve immediately with poached cherries and ice-cream.

POACHED CHERRIES Seed cherries. Combine sugar, rind, juice and the water in medium saucepan; stir over high heat, without boiling, until sugar dissolves. Bring to the boil, reduce heat; simmer, uncovered, 2 minutes. Add cherries, return to the boil. Reduce heat; simmer, covered, 2 minutes. Remove from heat; stir in liqueur. Cool.

prep + cook time 50 minutes (+ cooling) **serves** 6

frozen white chocolate mousse with espresso jelly and almond praline

2 eggs

250g (8 ounces) white eating chocolate

1 cup (250ml) thickened (heavy) cream

2 teaspoons vanilla extract

2 tablespoons caster (superfine) sugar

espresso jelly

2 tablespoons coffee-flavoured liqueur

1 cup (250ml) water

2 tablespoons caster (superfine) sugar

3 teaspoons instant espresso coffee

⅓ cup (80ml) boiling water

2½ teaspoons powdered gelatine

almond praline

½ cup (80g) blanched almonds

1 cup (220g) caster (superfine) sugar

½ cup (125ml) water

1 Have eggs at room temperature; separate eggs.
2 Cut eight 30cm (12-inch) squares of baking paper. Fold squares in half diagonally to form triangles. Hold the apex of the triangle towards you, then roll the paper into a cone shape, bringing the three points of the triangle together. Staple the three points together. Place cones in tall glasses or jugs.
3 Break chocolate into small saucepan, add ¼ cup of the cream; stir over low heat until smooth. Transfer to large bowl; cool 5 minutes. Stir in egg yolks.
4 Beat remaining cream and extract in small bowl with electric mixer until soft peaks form. Fold cream into chocolate mixture.
5 Beat egg whites and sugar in clean small bowl with electric mixer about 1 minute or until sugar is dissolved and soft peaks form. Fold egg whites into chocolate mixture, in two batches. Spoon mixture into paper cones. Freeze 6 hours or overnight until firm.
6 Meanwhile, make espresso jelly and almond praline.
7 Turn jelly onto board. Cut into 1cm (½-inch) cubes. Turn mousse cones onto serving plates, trimming bases to sit flat; discard paper cones. Spoon reserved coffee syrup onto plates, sprinkle with jelly and praline.

ESPRESSO JELLY Combine liqueur, the water and sugar in small saucepan; stir over high heat, without boiling, until sugar is dissolved. Stir in combined coffee and boiling water. Reserve ½ cup coffee syrup. Sprinkle gelatine over remaining coffee syrup in pan; stir over low heat until gelatine is dissolved. Cool 15 minutes. Rinse 15cm (6-inch) square cake pan with cold water; do not dry pan. Pour jelly into pan, cover; refrigerate about 2 hours or until jelly is set.

ALMOND PRALINE Preheat oven to 180°C/350°F. Place nuts, in single layer, on oven tray. Roast about 5 minutes or until browned lightly. Chop nuts coarsely; return to tray. Combine sugar and the water in small saucepan; stir over high heat, without boiling, until sugar dissolves. Bring to the boil; boil, uncovered, without stirring, about 10 minutes or until caramel in colour. Allow bubbles to subside. Pour toffee over nuts on tray; cool. Break praline into pieces.

prep + cook time 1½ hours (+ cooling, freezing & refrigeration) **serves** 8

tip If you have a coffee machine, use it to make three espresso coffees, rather than using instant coffee; you need ⅓ cup coffee.

flourless chocolate cake with mint toffee ice-cream

4 eggs

180g (5½ ounces) dark eating (semi-sweet) chocolate

100g (3 ounces) butter

⅓ cup (35g) cocoa powder

⅓ cup (80ml) hot water

1⅓ cups (300g) firmly packed light brown sugar

1 cup (120g) ground almonds

2 teaspoons cocoa powder, extra

¼ cup loosely packed fresh mint leaves

1.5 litres (6 cups) choc-mint ice-cream

toffee

1 cup (220g) caster (superfine) sugar

½ cup (125ml) water

1 Have eggs at room temperature; separate eggs.
2 Preheat oven to 160°C/325°F. Grease deep 25cm (10-inch) round cake pan; line base and side with baking paper.
3 Break chocolate into small saucepan. Chop butter, add to pan; stir over low heat until smooth. Remove from heat.
4 Blend sifted cocoa with the water in large bowl; whisk until smooth. Whisk in chocolate mixture, sugar, ground almonds and egg yolks until combined.
5 Beat egg whites in small bowl with electric mixer until soft peaks form. Fold into chocolate mixture, in two batches. Pour mixture into pan. Bake about 1 hour; cool cake in pan.
6 Meanwhile, make toffee.
7 Turn cake top-side up onto board. Dust cake with sifted extra cocoa. Cut cake into wedges with a hot dry knife.
8 Process toffee and mint leaves until finely chopped. Serve cake with scoops of ice-cream and mint toffee.

TOFFEE Grease oven tray. Combine sugar and the water in small saucepan; stir over high heat, without boiling, until sugar dissolves. Bring to the boil; boil, uncovered, without stirring, about 12 minutes or until light caramel in colour. Pour toffee onto tray; cool. Break toffee into pieces.

prep + cook time 1½ hours (+ cooling) serves 12

tips Cake and toffee can be made a day ahead. Store in separate airtight containers. Once the toffee is processed with the mint leaves, it will become sticky and must be used immediately. A 25cm (closed) springform pan can be used to make this cake.

chocolate panna cotta with rhubarb jelly

½ vanilla bean

150g (4½ ounces) dark eating (semi-sweet) chocolate

1¼ cups (310ml) pouring cream (see notes)

1 cup (250ml) milk

¼ cup (55g) caster (superfine) sugar

2 teaspoons powdered gelatine

rhubarb jelly

250g (8 ounces) trimmed rhubarb

½ cup (110g) caster (superfine) sugar

1¼ cups (310ml) water

2 teaspoons powdered gelatine

¼ cup (60ml) boiling water

pink food colouring

1 Make rhubarb jelly.

2 To make chocolate panna cotta: Split vanilla bean in half lengthways; scrape seeds into medium saucepan, add bean. Break chocolate into pan, add cream; stir over low heat until smooth. Stir in milk and sugar; stir until sugar dissolves. Sprinkle gelatine over mixture; stir until dissolved. Strain mixture through fine sieve into large jug; discard vanilla bean. Cool.

3 Pour panna cotta mixture over jelly; refrigerate overnight. Decorate with chocolate shapes just before serving. To make chocolate shapes, see notes.

RHUBARB JELLY Chop rhubarb coarsely. Stir sugar and the water in medium saucepan, over high heat, without boiling, until sugar is dissolved. Bring to the boil, add rhubarb; simmer about 10 minutes or until rhubarb is soft. Strain mixture through fine sieve into medium jug. Sprinkle gelatine over the boiling water in heatproof cup or jug; stir until dissolved. Stir gelatine mixture into rhubarb mixture. Tint pink with colouring. Pour into eight heatproof serving glasses. Refrigerate until set.

prep + cook time 55 minutes (+ refrigeration & cooling) **serves** 8

notes It is fine to use just the one 300ml carton of cream for this recipe.
To make chocolate shapes: Melt 50g (1½ ounces) dark chocolate; place into a resealable plastic bag. Cut a tiny snip off one corner, and pipe small shapes onto baking paper. Leave shapes to set at room temperature.

chocolate fondants with mascarpone coffee ice-cream

2 eggs

2 egg yolks

180g (5½ ounces) dark eating (semi-sweet) chocolate

125g (4 ounces) butter

⅓ cup (75g) caster (superfine) sugar

¼ cup (35g) plain (all-purpose) flour

90g (3 ounces) milk eating chocolate

¼ cup (60ml) pouring cream

2 teaspoons icing (confectioners') sugar

mascarpone coffee ice-cream

1½ tablespoons instant coffee granules

1½ tablespoons boiling water

1¼ cups (310ml) thickened (heavy) cream (see note)

1 cup (160g) icing (confectioners') sugar

250g (8 ounces) mascarpone

1 Have eggs and egg yolks at room temperature.

2 Make mascarpone coffee ice-cream.

3 Break dark chocolate into small saucepan. Chop butter, add to pan; stir over low heat until smooth. Transfer to medium bowl; cool 10 minutes.

4 Beat eggs, egg yolks and caster sugar in small bowl with electric mixer about 5 minutes or until thick and creamy. Fold egg mixture and sifted flour into dark chocolate mixture. Refrigerate 2 hours.

5 Preheat oven to 200°C/400°F. Grease six-hole (¾-cup/180ml) texas muffin pan well with butter. Spoon mixture into pan holes; bake fondants for 10 minutes.

6 Meanwhile, break milk chocolate into small saucepan, add cream; stir over low heat until sauce is smooth.

6 Lift ice-cream slab onto board. Using 8.5cm (3½-inch) round cutter, cut six rounds from ice-cream; place rounds on serving plates. Turn puddings out of pan; place on top of ice-cream rounds. Dust with sifted icing sugar; serve fondants immediately with chocolate sauce.

MASCARPONE COFFEE ICE-CREAM Line base of 18cm x 28cm (7-inch x 11-inch) slice pan with baking paper, extending paper 5cm (2 inches) over sides. Combine coffee and the water in small bowl; stir until coffee is dissolved. Beat cream and sifted icing sugar in small bowl with electric mixer until soft peaks form; fold in the coffee mixture and mascarpone. Spread mixture into pan; smooth surface. Cover with foil; freeze about 4 hours or overnight until firm.

prep + cook time 50 minutes (+ refrigeration & freezing) **serves** 6

note It is fine to use just one 300ml carton of cream for the mascarpone coffee ice-cream.

tip The uncooked fondant mixture thickens while chilling in the fridge for 2 hours; this method gives the best results because, when baking, the heat quickly sets the cold outside of the fondant, while the centre stays runny. These cakes must be eaten immediately, as the runny centre will thicken on standing and be absorbed into the sponge layer.

chocolate mousse cake with satin glaze and hazelnut mascarpone

2 eggs

360g (12 ounces) dark eating (semi-sweet) chocolate

¼ cup (55g) caster (superfine) sugar

2 tablespoons cocoa powder

1¼ cups (310ml) thickened (heavy) cream (see note)

¼ cup (40g) icing (confectioners') sugar

satin glaze

¼ cup (25g) cocoa powder

2 tablespoons water

80g (2½ ounces) dark eating (semi-sweet) chocolate

¼ cup (55g) caster (superfine) sugar

10g (½ ounce) butter

¼ cup (60ml) pouring cream

hazelnut mascarpone

⅓ cup (110g) chocolate-hazelnut spread

⅔ cup (170g) mascarpone

toffee hazelnuts

½ cup (110g) caster (superfine) sugar

¼ cup (60ml) water

8 roasted hazelnuts

1 Have eggs at room temperature; separate eggs.

2 Preheat oven to 180°C/350°F. Grease deep 20cm (8-inch) square cake pan; line base with baking paper.

3 Break 60g (2 ounces) of the chocolate into small heatproof bowl (don't let water touch base of bowl); stir over small saucepan of simmering water until smooth. Cool until just warm.

4 Beat egg whites and caster sugar in small bowl with electric mixer until sugar is dissolved. Beat in egg yolks. Fold in sifted cocoa, then melted chocolate. Spread mixture into pan. Bake about 10 minutes. Turn cake onto wire rack covered with baking paper, peel away lining paper; cool.

5 Grease cleaned deep 20cm (8-inch) square cake pan; line base and sides with baking paper, extending paper 5cm (2 inches) over sides. Place cake in pan.

6 Melt remaining chocolate in medium bowl over medium saucepan of simmering water; cool 10 minutes.

7 Beat cream and sifted icing sugar in small bowl with electric mixer until soft peaks form. Fold cream mixture into chocolate, in two batches. Spread mousse over cake in pan, smooth surface. Cover; refrigerate about 4 hours or until firm.

8 Make satin glaze. Spread glaze over mousse in pan. Refrigerate about 1 hour or until firm.

9 Make hazelnut mascarpone and toffee hazelnuts.

10 Lift mousse cake onto board. Trim edges with hot dry knife. Cut cake into eight rectangles; place on serving plates.

11 Top with hazelnut mascarpone and a toffee hazelnut.

SATIN GLAZE Blend sifted cocoa with the water in medium saucepan; stir until smooth. Break chocolate in pieces; add to cocoa mixture, stir in remaining ingredients; stir over low heat until smooth. Cool.

HAZELNUT MASCARPONE Fold spread through mascarpone.

TOFFEE HAZELNUTS Combine sugar and the water in small saucepan; stir over high heat, without boiling, until sugar dissolves. Bring to the boil; boil, uncovered, without stirring, about 4 minutes or until caramel in colour. Meanwhile, push a strong wooden toothpick into each hazelnut. Remove toffee from heat; allow bubbles to subside. Working with one nut at a time, hold nut by the toothpick, dip into the thickened toffee. Hold the nut above the toffee so that a trail of toffee falls from the nut. Hold the handle of a greased wooden spoon at the base of the toffee trail; quickly wind the toffee around the handle. Slowly withdraw the handle from the toffee spiral.

prep + cook time 1¾ hours (+ cooling & refrigeration) **serves** 8

note It is fine to use just the one 300ml carton of cream for this recipe.

chocolate mousse
with chocolate meringue crisps

2 eggs

250g (8 ounces) dark eating (semi-sweet) chocolate

1¼ cups (310ml) thickened (heavy) cream (see note)

2 tablespoons caster (superfine) sugar

chocolate meringue crisps

2 egg whites

½ cup (110g) caster (superfine) sugar

1½ tablespoons cocoa powder

2 tablespoons flaked almonds

1 Have eggs at room temperature; separate eggs.
2 Break chocolate into small saucepan, add ¼ cup of the cream; stir over low heat until smooth. Transfer to large bowl; cool 10 minutes. Stir in egg yolks.
3 Beat remaining cream in small bowl with electric mixer until soft peaks form. Fold cream into chocolate mixture.
4 Beat egg whites and sugar in clean small bowl with electric mixer until sugar is dissolved. Fold into chocolate mixture, in two batches.
5 Spoon mousse into six ¾-cup (180ml) serving glasses. Refrigerate about 1 hour or overnight until set. (If refrigerated overnight, stand at room temperature for about 20 minutes before serving to allow mixture to soften.)
6 Meanwhile, make chocolate meringue crisps.
7 Serve mousse accompanied with meringue crisps.

CHOCOLATE MERINGUE CRISPS
Preheat oven to 120°C/250°F. Line large oven tray with baking paper. Beat egg whites and sugar in small bowl with electric mixer until sugar is dissolved. Beat in sifted cocoa on low speed. Spread mixture into six 5cm x 12cm (2-inch x 4¾-inch) rectangles, about 5cm (2 inches) apart, on tray; sprinkle with nuts. Bake about 40 minutes or until dry to touch. Cool in oven with door ajar.

prep + cook time 1½ hours (+ cooling & refrigeration)
serves 6

note It is fine to use just the one 300ml carton of cream for this recipe.

tip To make the crisps uniform, draw rectangles on baking paper, turn the paper over, then pipe meringue into the rectangular shapes. Spread mixture evenly with a metal spatula. Trim edges of cold crisps with a sharp knife.

white chocolate meringue torte with white peaches

6 egg whites

1½ cups (330g) caster (superfine) sugar

¼ teaspoon cream of tartar

½ teaspoon vanilla extract

1 teaspoon white vinegar

2 teaspoons cornflour (cornstarch)

white chocolate cream

180g (5½ ounces) white eating chocolate

2 cups (500ml) thickened (heavy) cream

1 tablespoon orange-flavoured liqueur

2 tablespoons icing (confectioners') sugar

liqueur peaches

4 large white peaches (880g)

¼ cup (60ml) orange-flavoured liqueur

¼ cup (55g) caster (superfine) sugar

1 Have egg whites at room temperature.

2 Preheat oven to 100°C/210°F. Line three large oven trays with baking paper. Mark 12cm x 30cm (5-inch x 12-inch) rectangle on each piece of paper; turn paper, marked-side down, on trays.

3 Beat egg whites, sugar and cream of tartar in medium bowl with electric mixer about 8 minutes or until sugar is dissolved and firm peaks form. Beat in extract, vinegar and cornflour.

4 Divide meringue evenly between marked rectangles; spread meringue to just inside marked lines. Bake meringues about 40 minutes or until dry to touch. Cool in oven with door ajar.

5 Make white chocolate cream and liqueur peaches.

6 Place one layer of meringue on serving plate. Spread with half the white chocolate cream. Repeat layering, finishing with meringue.

7 Serve meringue torte with liqueur peaches.

WHITE CHOCOLATE CREAM Break chocolate into small saucepan, add ¼ cup of the cream; stir over low heat until smooth. Transfer to large bowl, cool. Beat remaining cream, liqueur and sifted icing sugar in small bowl with electric mixer until soft peaks form. Fold into chocolate mixture, in two batches.

LIQUEUR PEACHES Make a small cross in skin of peaches at stem end. Place peaches in large heatproof bowl; cover with boiling water. Stand 30 seconds; drain. Peel away skins. Halve peaches; remove stones. Slice peaches into wedges. Combine peach slices, liqueur and sugar in large bowl; toss gently. Stand about 20 minutes or until sugar is dissolved, stirring occasionally.

prep + cook time 1½ hours (+ cooling & standing) **serves** 8

vanilla white chocolate syllabub with berries

1 vanilla bean

¾ cup (180ml) sweet dessert wine

¼ cup (55g) caster (superfine) sugar

1 tablespoon lemon juice

180g (5½ ounces) white eating chocolate

1¼ cups (310ml) thick (double) cream (see note)

750g (1½ pounds) mixed fresh berries

1 To make syllabub: Split vanilla bean lengthways, scrape seeds into small saucepan; add bean, ½ cup of the wine and 2 tablespoons of the sugar. Stir over high heat, without boiling, until sugar dissolves. Bring to the boil; boil, uncovered, about 5 minutes or until reduced by half. Stir in juice; transfer to medium heatproof bowl, cool. Cover; refrigerate 1 hour.
2 Meanwhile, break chocolate into small saucepan, add ¼ cup of the cream; stir over low heat until smooth. Transfer mixture to large heatproof bowl; cool to room temperature.
3 Combine remaining wine and sugar, and berries in medium bowl; stand 15 minutes.
4 Discard vanilla bean from wine mixture. Gently whisk remaining cream into wine mixture. Fold cream mixture into chocolate mixture, in two batches.
5 Divide berry mixture between six 1-cup (250ml) serving glasses; top with syllabub.

prep + cook time 40 minutes (+ cooling, standing & refrigeration) **serves** 6

note It is fine to use just the one 300ml carton of cream for this recipe.

chocolate gelato terrine with honeycomb and chocolate fudge sauce

1 litre (4 cups) dark chocolate gelato

1 litre (4 cups) vanilla ice-cream

honeycomb

¾ cup (165g) white (granulated) sugar

1 tablespoon golden syrup or treacle

¼ cup (60ml) water

1½ teaspoons bicarbonate of soda (baking soda)

chocolate fudge sauce

180g (5½ ounces) dark eating (semi-sweet) chocolate

30g (1 ounce) butter

1 cup (250ml) pouring cream

¼ cup (40g) icing (confectioners') sugar

1 Line base and long sides of 10.5cm x 23.5cm (4-inch x 9½-inch) (top measurement) loaf pan or terrine with baking paper or foil, extending paper 5cm (2 inches) over sides.
2 Press barely-softened chocolate gelato into pan; smooth surface. Cover; freeze about 1 hour or until firm.
3 Meanwhile, make honeycomb.
4 Stir half the honeycomb pieces into barely-softened vanilla gelato; press over chocolate gelato in pan, smooth surface. Cover; freeze about 2 hours or until firm.
5 Make chocolate fudge sauce.
6 Turn gelato terrine onto board; peel away lining paper. Cut terrine into eight slices. Serve with remaining honeycomb and warm fudge sauce.

HONEYCOMB Line oven tray with baking paper. Combine sugar, syrup and the water in small saucepan; stir over high heat, without boiling, until sugar dissolves. Bring to the boil; boil, uncovered, without stirring, about 8 minutes or until syrup reaches 154°C/309°F (hard crack) on a candy thermometer. (Or, a small spoonful will snap when dropped into a cup of cold water.) Remove from heat, stir in sifted soda; the mixture will foam. Pour mixture onto tray without spreading; stand about 1 hour or until firm. Break honeycomb into pieces; store in an airtight container.

CHOCOLATE FUDGE SAUCE Break chocolate into medium saucepan. Chop butter; add butter and cream to pan, stir over low heat until smooth. Remove from heat; gradually whisk in sifted icing sugar.

prep + cook time 40 minutes (+ freezing & standing) serves 8

notes Be aware that the honeycomb will foam up very quickly once the bicarbonate of soda is added. Store the honeycomb in an airtight container in a cool dry place at room temperature for up to 2 days. Candy thermometers are available from kitchenware stores. Digital thermometers are easier to read.
The recipe can be made a day ahead; reheat sauce over a low heat before serving.
If you have one, use a silicone loaf pan – its smooth surface means there's no need to line it and, with its sharp corners, the terrine is easy to turn out. If you prefer, use either ice-cream or gelato for both layers.

fruit desserts

honey and saffron pears

6 small firm pears (1kg)

¼ cup (60ml) lemon juice

¼ teaspoon saffron threads

1 cup (350g) honey

2 cups (500ml) water

¾ cup (165g) caster (superfine) sugar

¼ cup (60ml) water, extra

1 Peel pears; place in large bowl, cover with cold water, stir in juice.
2 Dry-fry saffron in a medium saucepan (large enough to fit the upright pears), stirring, over low heat about 1 minute or until fragrant. Add honey and the water; bring to the boil. Reduce heat; simmer, uncovered, 3 minutes. Add drained pears; simmer, covered until pears are just tender. Remove pears with slotted spoon to medium bowl; cool pears. Bring honey mixture to the boil; boil, uncovered, until liquid is reduced by half. Cool syrup.
3 Meanwhile, combine sugar and the extra water in small saucepan; stir over high heat, without boiling, until sugar dissolves. Bring to the boil. Reduce heat; simmer, uncovered, without stirring, until caramel in colour. Remove from heat; allow bubbles to subside.
4 To make toffee nests; place a sheet of baking paper on bench. Dip 2 forks into toffee; working over paper, with forks back to back, quickly pull the forks back and forth against each other to make thin strands of toffee. Working quickly, gather up the strands and shape into a nest. Place nest on serving plate. Repeat with remaining toffee to make 5 more nests.
5 Sit a pear in the middle of each nest; drizzle with honey syrup. Serve immediately.

prep + cook time 45 minutes (+ cooling) **serves** 6

tip The toffee nests can be made up to an hour before serving if the weather is cool.

peach melba cheesecakes

250g (8 ounces) cream cheese

90g (3 ounces) butter

200g (6½ ounces) shortbread biscuits

1 teaspoon powdered gelatine

1 tablespoon water

⅓ cup (80ml) lemon juice

2 tablespoons caster (superfine) sugar

395g (12½ ounces) canned sweetened condensed milk

1 teaspoon vanilla extract

1¼ cups (310ml) thickened (heavy) cream (see notes)

poached peaches

1 cup (220g) caster (superfine) sugar

2 cups (500ml) water

4 medium peaches (600g)

strawberry sauce

250g (8 ounces) strawberries

2 tablespoons caster (superfine) sugar

2 tablespoons redcurrant jelly

2 tablespoons water

1 Have cream cheese at room temperature. Grease 8 holes of a 12-hole (¾-cup/180ml) loose-based, straight-sided cheesecake pan.

2 Melt butter. Process biscuits until fine. Add butter; process until combined. Divide mixture evenly into pan holes, press firmly over base of pan using the bottom of a glass. Refrigerate 20 minutes.

3 Add gelatine to the water, in small heatproof jug, stand jug in small saucepan of simmering water; stir until gelatine is dissolved. Cool.

4 Beat cream cheese, juice, sugar, condensed milk and extract in small bowl with electric mixer until smooth. Transfer to large bowl; stir in gelatine mixture.

5 Beat cream in small bowl with electric mixer until soft peaks form; fold into cream cheese mixture. Spoon mixture into pan holes, smooth tops. Cover; refrigerate overnight.

6 Make poached peaches and strawberry sauce.

7 Remove cheesecakes from pan, place on serving plates; top with peaches, drizzle with sauce.

POACHED PEACHES
Combine sugar and the water in medium saucepan; stir over high heat, without boiling, until sugar dissolves. Simmer, uncovered, 2 minutes. Add whole peaches; simmer, uncovered, about 10 minutes or until peaches are tender and skins start to come away. Remove peaches with slotted spoon; cool. Peel away skins, halve peaches; discard stones. Cut peaches into wedges. Place peaches in medium bowl; add ½ cup of the poaching liquid. Refrigerate 20 minutes.

STRAWBERRY SAUCE Hull and halve strawberries. Combine strawberries, sugar, jelly and the water in medium saucepan; stir over low heat until sugar dissolves. Simmer, uncovered, about 5 minutes or until strawberries are soft. Push sauce through fine sieve into medium jug; discard seeds.

prep + cook time 45 minutes (+ refrigeration) **makes** 8

note Redcurrant jelly is a preserve found in the jam section of large supermarkets. It is fine to use just one 300ml carton of cream for this recipe. A cheesecake pan is similar to a texas muffin pan, only the bases are removable.

orange soufflés with caramelised oranges

60g (2 ounces) butter

⅔ cup (150g) caster (superfine) sugar

2 tablespoons water

2 teaspoons cornflour (cornstarch)

⅓ cup (80ml) strained orange juice

4 egg whites

2 tablespoons caster (superfine) sugar, extra

2 tablespoons icing (confectioners') sugar

caramelised oranges

4 medium oranges (960g)

1 cup (220g) caster (superfine) sugar

1 vanilla bean

1 Make caramelised oranges.
2 Preheat oven to 200°C/400°F. Melt the butter and use to grease six ¾-cup (180ml) ovenproof soufflé dishes; sprinkle with 2 tablespoons of the caster sugar, shake out excess sugar. Place dishes on oven tray.
3 Combine the remaining caster sugar and the water in small saucepan; stir over high heat, without boiling, until sugar dissolves. Bring to the boil. Reduce heat; simmer, uncovered, without stirring, 2 minutes.
4 Blend cornflour with the juice in small bowl, add to sugar syrup; cook, stirring, over high heat, until mixture boils and thickens. Boil 1 minute, stirring.
5 Beat egg whites and extra caster sugar in small bowl with electric mixer until soft peaks form; transfer to large bowl. Fold warm sugar syrup mixture into egg white mixture.
6 Spoon mixture evenly into dishes; smooth surface. Bake soufflés about 15 minutes. Dust with sifted icing sugar; serve soufflés immediately with caramelised oranges.

CARAMELISED ORANGES Peel oranges thickly to remove all white pith; cut each orange crossways into 4 slices. Place sugar in large frying pan; cook, over medium heat, without stirring, until it turns a dark caramel colour (tilt the pan during cooking). Split and scrape seeds from vanilla bean into pan; add bean and orange slices. Gently shake pan to coat oranges in caramel. Cook 1 minute. Remove pan from heat; stand 2 minutes. Transfer orange slices and any soft caramel from the pan to medium heatproof bowl. Cover; refrigerate 2 hours. (The caramel will soften to form a syrup.) Discard vanilla bean before serving.

prep + cook time 35 minutes (+ refrigeration) **serves** 6

notes The oranges can be prepared up to 2 days before serving. Store, covered, in the refrigerator. Swirl, don't stir, the toffee; this will encourage uniform melting and colouring of the sugar.

pear and marzipan tartlets

¾ cup (165g) caster (superfine) sugar

2½ cups (625ml) water

1 tablespoon maple syrup

1 vanilla bean

12 baby pears (1.2kg)

3 sheets ready-rolled puff pastry

1 egg white, beaten lightly

marzipan

¾ cup (120g) pure icing (confectioners') sugar

1 cup (120g) ground almonds

1 egg white

maple vanilla syrup

¼ cup (55g) caster (superfine) sugar

1 tablespoon maple syrup

1 Combine sugar, the water, syrup and scraped vanilla bean in medium saucepan. Stir over high heat, without boiling, until sugar is dissolved. Bring to the boil, reduce heat, simmer.

2 Preheat oven to 200°C/400°F.

3 Peel pears, add to simmering syrup mixture; simmer, uncovered, about 15 minutes or until pears are barely tender. Remove from heat; cool to room temperature. Drain pears; reserve ½ cup poaching liquid for the maple vanilla syrup.

4 Meanwhile, make marzipan.

5 Using 8cm (3¼-inch) round cutter, cut 24 rounds from pastry sheets. Place 12 rounds onto baking-paper-lined oven trays. Using 5cm (2-inch) round cutter, cut holes in centres of remaining 12 pastry rounds. Brush rounds on trays with egg white; top with pastry rings. Brush rings with more egg white.

6 Roll marzipan out on surface lightly dusted with icing sugar to 5mm (¼-inch) thickness. Using 4.5cm (1¾-inch) round cutter, cut 12 rounds from marzipan. Place rounds inside rings of pastry.

7 Top marzipan with pears, pushing down gently. Bake about 20 minutes or until pastry is golden brown.

8 Meanwhile, make maple vanilla syrup; pour hot syrup over hot tartlets. Cool, before serving with cream, if you like.

MARZIPAN Sift icing sugar and ground almonds into small bowl, add egg white. Use fork to combine ingredients. Press together to make a smooth ball.

MAPLE VANILLA SYRUP Combine reserved poaching liquid, sugar and syrup in small saucepan; stir over high heat until sugar is dissolved. Bring to the boil; reduce heat, simmer about 10 minutes.

prep + cook time 1 hour (+ refrigeration) **makes** 12

tips We used Paradise pears. Corella pears are also good. These tarts are best made on the day of serving.

caramel and cream banana tarts

185g (6 ounces) cold butter

2 cups (300g) plain (all-purpose) flour

2 tablespoons icing (confectioners') sugar

1 egg yolk

1 teaspoon vanilla extract

2 teaspoons iced water, approximately

1 cup (250ml) double (thick) cream

caramel filling

1¼ cups (310ml) pouring cream (see note)

½ cup (110g) firmly packed light brown sugar

30g (1 ounce) butter

toffee bananas

1 cup (220g) caster (superfine) sugar

½ cup (125ml) water

2 medium bananas (260g)

1 Make caramel filling.

2 Preheat oven to 200°C/400°F. Grease eight 8.5cm (3½-inch) individual brioche pans or loose-based tart pans.

3 Chop cold butter coarsely; combine in processor with flour and icing sugar, process until crumbly. With the motor operating, add egg yolk, extract and enough of the water to make ingredients cling together. Knead dough on floured surface until smooth. Enclose in plastic wrap; refrigerate 30 minutes.

4 Divide pastry into eight equal portions. Roll out each portion on floured surface until large enough to line pans. Lift pastry into pans; press over bases and sides, trim excess pastry. Prick bases all over with fork; place pans on oven tray. Bake about 10 minutes or until browned lightly. Cool in pans.

5 Meanwhile, make toffee bananas.

6 Carefully turn tart shells out of pans, place on serving plates. Spoon caramel filling into tart shells, top with cream, then toffee bananas. Serve immediately.

CARAMEL FILLING Combine ingredients in medium saucepan; stir over medium heat until smooth. Simmer, uncovered, about 10 minutes, stirring, until mixture is thick and caramel in colour. Cool.

TOFFEE BANANAS Line oven tray with baking paper. Stir sugar and the water in medium saucepan over high heat, without boiling, until sugar dissolves. Bring to the boil; boil, uncovered, without stirring, until pale caramel in colour. Remove from heat; allow bubbles to subside. Peel bananas, slice thinly diagonally. Using a fork, carefully dip each slice of banana into toffee, place on tray. Stand at room temperature until set.

prep + cook time 35 minutes (+ refrigeration, cooling & standing) **makes** 8

note It is fine to use just one 300ml carton of cream for the caramel filling.

raspberry rose meringues

250g (8 ounces) fresh raspberries

4 egg whites

1 teaspoon rosewater

1 cup (220g) caster (superfine) sugar

⅓ cup (100g) redcurrant jelly

2 tablespoons caster (superfine) sugar, extra

1¼ cups (310ml) thickened (heavy) cream, whipped (see notes)

1 Preheat oven to 120°C/250°F. Line oven tray with baking paper.
2 Push half the berries through a fine sieve over small bowl; discard seeds. Reserve 2 tablespoons of the puree.
3 Beat egg whites, rosewater and sugar in small bowl with electric mixer, on high speed, about 10 minutes or until sugar is dissolved. Add reserved raspberry puree; gently swirl to marble mixture. Divide mixture into four mounds, about 5cm (2 inches) apart, on tray; use the back of a spoon to shape mounds into nests. Bake meringues about 35 minutes or until dry to touch. Cool in oven with door ajar.
4 Meanwhile, combine remaining puree, jelly and extra sugar in small saucepan; stir over low heat until smooth. Bring to the boil. Reduce heat; simmer, uncovered, about 3 minutes or until thickened slightly. Transfer to small jug; cool.
5 Serve meringues topped with whipped cream; drizzle with raspberry sauce, top with remaining raspberries.

prep + cook time 45 minutes (+ cooling) **serves** 4

notes It is fine to use just the one 300ml carton of cream for this recipe. The meringues are best eaten within 2 hours of baking. Use strawberries or blackberries in place of the raspberries. Redcurrant jelly is a preserve found in the jam section of large supermarkets.

vanilla cherries with chocolate blancmange

¼ cup (35g) cornflour (cornstarch)

2 tablespoons cocoa powder

2 tablespoons caster (superfine) sugar

1¼ cups (310ml) milk

1¼ cups (310ml) pouring cream (see note)

1 teaspoon vanilla extract

1 vanilla bean

½ cup (110g) caster (superfine) sugar, extra

¾ cup (180ml) water

500g (1 pound) fresh cherries

1 Sift cornflour, cocoa and sugar into medium saucepan; gradually stir in milk and cream. Cook, stirring, over medium heat, until mixture boils and thickens. Reduce heat; simmer, stirring, 2 minutes. Remove from heat; stir in extract.

2 Spoon mixture into six serving glasses; cover surface with plastic wrap. Refrigerate 3 hours.

3 Split vanilla bean, scrape seeds into medium saucepan, add bean, extra sugar and the water; stir over high heat, without boiling, until sugar dissolves. Bring to the boil. Reduce heat; simmer, uncovered, about 10 minutes or until syrup is slightly thickened.

4 Transfer syrup to medium heatproof bowl, add cherries, cover; refrigerate 1 hour. Serve blancmange topped with cherry and syrup mixture.

prep + cook time 35 minutes (+ refrigeration) **serves** 6

notes It is fine to use just one 300ml carton of cream for this recipe.
The fresh cherries still have their seeds, so be careful when eating.

pear and marshmallow trifles

3 eggs

¾ cup (165g) caster (superfine) sugar

1 cup (150g) self-raising flour

3 medium pears (630g)

½ cup (110g) caster (superfine) sugar, extra

2 cups (500ml) water

1 medium orange (240g)

¼ cup (30g) coarsely chopped roasted unsalted pistachios

6 x 3cm x 4cm (1¼-inch x 1½-inch) sheets edible gold leaf

marshmallow

1 cup (220g) caster (superfine) sugar

¾ cup (180ml) water

3 teaspoons powdered gelatine

2 tablespoons water, extra

1 Have eggs at room temperature.

2 Preheat oven to 180°C/350°F. Grease 20cm x 30cm (8-inch x 12-inch) rectangular pan; line base and long sides with baking paper, extending paper 5cm (2 inches) over sides.

3 Beat eggs and sugar in small bowl with electric mixer until thick and creamy and sugar is dissolved. Transfer mixture to large bowl. Sift flour over egg mixture and fold ingredients together. Pour mixture into pan; bake about 30 minutes. Turn sponge immediately, top-side up, onto baking-paper-covered wire rack to cool.

4 Meanwhile, peel, quarter and core pears.

5 Combine extra sugar and the water in medium saucepan. Using vegetable peeler, remove 5cm (2-inch) strip of rind from orange; juice orange (you need ¼ cup juice). Add rind and juice to pan; stir over high heat, without boiling, until sugar dissolves. Bring to the boil, reduce heat; simmer, uncovered, 3 minutes. Add pear; simmer, uncovered, until pear is barely tender. Cool pear in poaching liquid.

6 Make marshmallow.

7 Cut cake into 2cm (¾-inch) cubes, divide between 6 serving glasses; sprinkle each with a tablespoon of pear poaching liquid, top with pears. Spoon marshmallow mixture into glasses; sprinkle with nuts. Use tweezers to lift pieces of gold leaf onto stems of pears; wrap around stems gently, being careful not to touch the gold leaf with your hands, as it will stick.

MARSHMALLOW Combine sugar and the water in medium saucepan; stir over high heat, without boiling, until sugar dissolves. Bring to the boil, reduce heat; simmer, uncovered, without stirring, until syrup reaches 115°C/240°F on a candy thermometer. Meanwhile, sprinkle gelatine over the extra water in small bowl; stand mixture 5 minutes. Stir gelatine mixture into hot syrup; transfer mixture to medium heatproof bowl, cool until mixture is only just warm. Beat sugar syrup with electric mixer about 8 minutes or until thick and glossy.

prep + cook time 45 minutes (+ cooling & refrigeration) **makes** 6

note Edible gold leaf and candy thermometers are available from kitchenware stores and cake decorating suppliers.

coconut panna cotta with caramelised mango and coconut wafers

1¼ cups (310ml) pouring cream (see notes)

½ cup (110g) caster (superfine) sugar

2 tablespoons powdered gelatine

⅓ cup (80ml) boiling water

375g (12 ounces) greek-style vanilla yogurt

1 teaspoon coconut extract

coconut wafers

1 sheet frozen puff pastry

1 egg white

½ cup (40g) desiccated coconut

caramelised mangoes

2 medium mangoes (860g)

⅓ cup (75g) caster (superfine) sugar

1 Combine cream and sugar in medium saucepan; stir over high heat, without boiling, until sugar dissolves. Sprinkle gelatine over the boiling water in small heatproof jug, stand jug in small saucepan of simmering water; stir until gelatine dissolves. Stir gelatine mixture into hot cream mixture. Transfer to medium bowl; cool.

2 Stir yogurt and extract into cooled cream mixture.

3 Rinse eight ¾-cup (180ml) moulds with cold water; drain, do not wipe dry. Pour yogurt mixture into moulds, cover loosely with plastic wrap; refrigerate 4 hours or until set.

4 Make coconut wafers and caramelised mangoes.

5 Carefully turn panna cottas onto serving plates. Serve with mangoes and wafers.

COCONUT WAFERS Preheat oven to 200°C/400°F. Grease and line oven tray with baking paper. Cut pastry in half, cut each half into four triangles; place on oven tray. Bake about 10 minutes. Remove from oven, brush with egg white, sprinkle with coconut. Bake a further 5 minutes or until coconut is golden.

CARAMELISED MANGOES Remove cheeks from mangoes; using large metal spoon, scoop flesh from skin. Sprinkle cut surfaces of mango cheeks with sugar. Heat large frying pan; cook mango, cut-side down, about 2 minutes or until caramelised. Remove from pan; cool, then slice thinly.

prep + cook time 45 minutes (+ cooling & refrigeration)
serves 8

notes It is fine to use just the one 300ml carton of cream for this recipe.

passionfruit jelly with poached pineapple

12 passionfruit

¾ cup (180ml) fresh orange juice, strained

¼ cup (60ml) fresh lemon juice, strained

¾ cup (165g) caster (superfine) sugar

1 cup (250ml) water

2 tablespoons powdered gelatine

⅓ cup (80ml) boiling water

½ cup (40g) flaked coconut or shaved fresh coconut, toasted

poached pineapple

1 small pineapple (900g)

1 cup (220g) caster (superfine) sugar

1 cup (250ml) water

10cm (4-inch) stick fresh lemon grass (20g)

4 fresh kaffir lime leaves

1 Halve passionfruit; scoop pulp into fine sieve over 2-cup measuring jug. Press to extract as much juice as possible. Discard seeds. Add orange and lemon juice to passionfruit juice, you should have 2 cups of juice.

2 Combine juice, sugar and the water in medium saucepan; stir over high heat, without boiling, until sugar dissolves. Bring to the boil; remove from heat.

3 Sprinkle gelatine over the boiling water in small heatproof jug. Stand jug in small saucepan of simmering water; stir until gelatine dissolves. Stir gelatine mixture into juice mixture.

4 Pour juice mixture into six 1-cup (250ml) serving glasses. Cover; refrigerate about 4 hours or until set.

5 Meanwhile, make poached pineapple.

6 Serve jellies topped with poached pineapple and coconut.

POACHED PINEAPPLE Peel pineapple; halve lengthways. Slice each half into very thin slices. Combine sugar and the water in medium saucepan; stir over high heat, without boiling, until sugar dissolves. Halve lemon grass lengthways, add to syrup with crushed lime leaves; bring to the boil. Reduce heat; simmer, uncovered, 5 minutes. Add pineapple; simmer, uncovered about 3 minutes or until pineapple is tender. Transfer pineapple mixture to medium heatproof bowl. Cover, refrigerate about 2 hours.

prep + cook time 25 minutes (+ refrigeration) **serves** 6

tip To toast the coconut, stir coconut in a medium frying pan, over low heat, about 3 minutes or until golden. Remove coconut from the pan immediately to prevent over-browning. Fresh coconut can be shaved into long flakes using a vegetable peeler.

pies & tarts

frangipane tart with caramelised figs

150g (4½ ounces) cold butter

1⅓ cups (200g) plain (all-purpose) flour

2 tablespoons iced water, approximately

5 medium fresh figs (300g)

2 tablespoons caster (superfine) sugar

¼ cup (80g) fig jam (conserve)

2 tablespoons water, extra

frangipane

150g (4½ ounces) butter

¾ cup (165g) caster (superfine) sugar

3 eggs

1½ cups (180g) ground almonds

⅓ cup (50g) plain (all-purpose) flour

1 Have butter for almond frangipane at room temperature.
2 Chop cold butter. Sift flour into large bowl; rub in butter until crumbly. Mix in enough of the water to make ingredients just come together. Knead dough lightly on floured surface until smooth. Flatten pastry slightly, wrap in plastic wrap; refrigerate 30 minutes.
3 Grease 11cm x 34cm (4½-inch x 13½-inch) loose-based fluted flan pan. Roll out pastry on floured surface or between sheets of baking paper until large enough to line pan.
4 Lift pastry into pan; press over base and sides, trim excess pastry. Prick base all over with fork; refrigerate 30 minutes.
5 Preheat oven to 200°C/400°F.
6 Place flan pan on oven tray, line pastry with baking paper; fill with dried beans or rice. Bake 15 minutes; remove paper and beans. Bake pastry a further 10 minutes.
7 Meanwhile, make frangipane.
8 Spread frangipane into tart shell; smooth surface. Bake about 25 minutes or until browned lightly; cool in pan.
9 Meanwhile, halve figs; sprinkle cut surface with sugar. Heat large frying pan; place figs, cut-side down, in pan. Cook over medium heat until figs are caramelised. Remove figs from pan. Add jam and the extra water to pan; cook, stirring, until syrupy.
10 Place tart on serving plate; pour over warm syrup, top with figs. Serve with double or whipped cream, if you like.

FRANGIPANE Whisk butter and sugar in medium bowl until light and fluffy; whisk in eggs, one at a time, until combined. Stir in ground almonds and sifted flour until combined.

prep + cook time 1½ hours (+ refrigeration & cooling)
serves 10

tips You can also make the pastry in a food processor. Process flour and butter until crumbly; with motor operating, add the water, process until ingredients just come together. Or you can use ready-made shortcrust pastry.

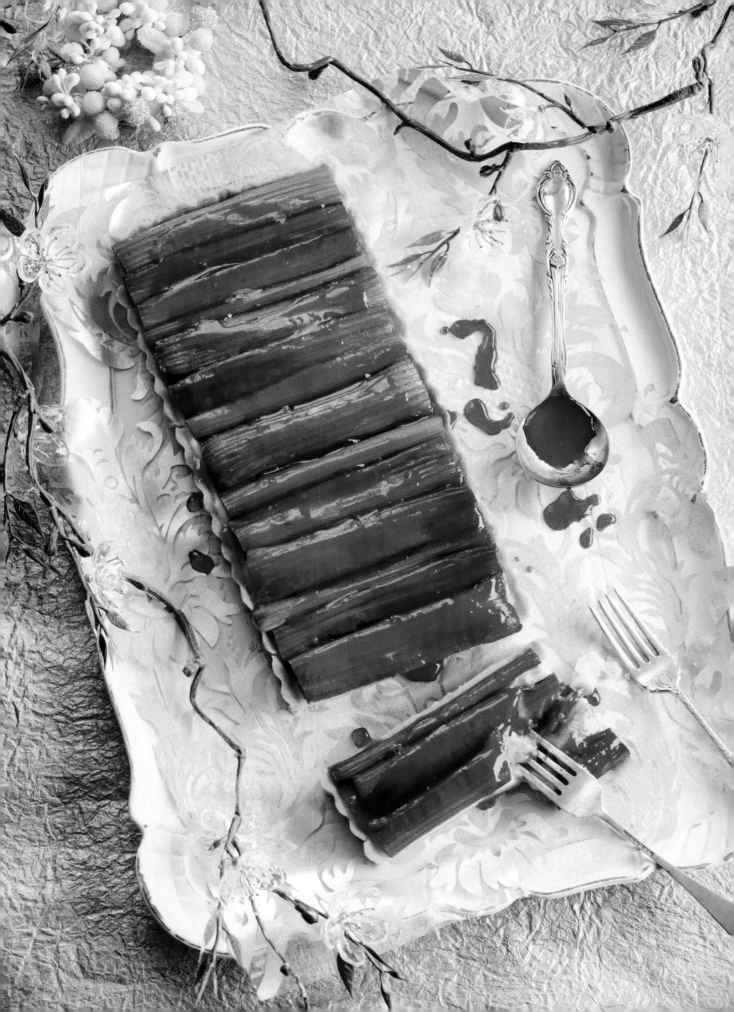

roasted rhubarb custard tart

150g (4½ ounces) cold butter

1⅓ cups (200g) plain (all-purpose) flour

2 tablespoons iced water, approximately

1 bunch rhubarb (500g)

2 tablespoons icing (confectioners') sugar

vanilla pastry cream

1 vanilla bean

2 cups (500ml) milk

5 egg yolks

½ cup (110g) caster (superfine) sugar

⅓ cup (50g) cornflour (cornstarch)

50g (1½ ounces) butter

1 Make vanilla pastry cream.
2 Chop cold butter. Sift flour into large bowl; rub in butter until crumbly. Mix in enough of the water to make ingredients just come together. Knead dough lightly on floured surface until smooth. Flatten pastry slightly, wrap in plastic wrap; refrigerate 30 minutes.
3 Grease 11cm x 34cm (4½-inch x 13½-inch) loose-based fluted flan pan. Roll out pastry on floured surface or between sheets of baking paper until large enough to line pan.
4 Lift pastry into pan; press over base and sides, trim excess pastry. Prick base all over with fork; refrigerate 30 minutes.
5 Preheat oven to 200°C/400°F.
6 Place flan pan on oven tray, line pastry with baking paper; fill with dried beans or rice. Bake 15 minutes; remove paper and beans. Bake a further 10 minutes or until pastry is browned lightly and crisp; cool.
7 Trim rhubarb; cut stems into 11cm sticks. Toss rhubarb with icing sugar in shallow baking dish. Roast, uncovered, about 10 minutes or until rhubarb is tender but still holds its shape; cool. Drain rhubarb; reserve syrup in dish.
8 Spread pastry cream into tart shell; top with rhubarb, drizzle with syrup. Serve immediately.

VANILLA PASTRY CREAM Split vanilla bean lengthways, scrape seeds into small saucepan, add bean and milk. Bring to the boil; remove from heat. Whisk egg yolks, sugar and cornflour in medium heatproof bowl until combined; gradually whisk in hot milk mixture. Strain into same saucepan; discard vanilla bean. Whisk over high heat until mixture boils and thickens. Remove from heat; whisk in butter. Transfer to medium bowl, cover surface with plastic wrap; refrigerate about 1 hour or until cool.

prep + cook time 1¾ hours (+ refrigeration & cooling)
serves 8

tips You can also make the pastry using a food processor. Process flour and butter until crumbly; with motor operating, add the water and process until ingredients just come together. Or you can use ready-made shortcrust pastry.
If you don't have a rectangular flan pan, use a 22cm (9-inch) round flan pan.
If the pastry cream is difficult to spread, beat it with an electric mixer until smooth before filling the tart shell.

ruby grapefruit meringue pies

185g (6 ounces) cold butter

1⅔ cups (250g) plain (all-purpose) flour

¼ cup (60ml) iced water, approximately

meringue

⅓ cup (75g) caster (superfine) sugar

¼ cup (60ml) water

2 egg whites

pinch cream of tartar

ruby grapefruit curd

5 egg yolks

¾ cup (165g) caster (superfine) sugar

75g (2½ ounces) butter

2 teaspoons finely grated ruby red grapefruit rind

½ cup (125ml) fresh ruby red grapefruit juice

1 Make ruby grapefruit curd.
2 Chop cold butter. Sift flour into large bowl; rub in butter until crumbly. Mix in enough of the water to make ingredients just come together. Knead dough lightly on floured surface until smooth. Flatten pastry slightly, wrap in plastic wrap; refrigerate 30 minutes.
3 Grease eight 8cm (3¼-inch) round loose-based fluted flan pans. Divide pastry into eight equal portions. Roll out each portion on floured surface or between sheets of baking paper until large enough to line pans.
4 Lift pastry into pans; press into bases and sides, trim excess pastry. Prick bases all over with fork, place pans on oven tray; refrigerate 30 minutes.
5 Preheat oven to 200°C/400°F.
6 Line pastry with baking paper; fill with dried beans or rice. Bake, on oven tray, 15 minutes; remove paper and beans. Bake a further 10 minutes or until browned lightly and crisp. Cool.
7 Spread curd into tart shells.
8 Make meringue.
9 Spoon meringue into piping bag fitted with large 1.5cm (¾-inch) plain tube; pipe meringue onto tarts. Serve immediately or brown lightly with a blowtorch, if you like.

RUBY GRAPEFRUIT CURD Whisk egg yolks and sugar in medium heatproof bowl over medium saucepan of simmering water. Chop butter, add to pan with rind and juice. Cook, stirring, until mixture coats the back of a spoon. Pour into clean medium heatproof bowl, cover surface with plastic wrap; refrigerate until cool.

MERINGUE Combine sugar and the water in small saucepan; stir over high heat, without boiling, until sugar dissolves. Bring to the boil. Reduce heat; simmer, uncovered, without stirring, until syrup reaches 115°C/240°F on a candy thermometer. When syrup reaches 115°C, start beating egg whites with cream of tartar in medium bowl with electric mixer until soft peaks form. While beating egg whites, bring sugar syrup to 121°C/250°F. With motor operating, gradually pour syrup into egg whites in a thin steady stream; continue beating until mixture is thick, glossy and cooled to room temperature.

prep + cook time 1½ hours (+ cooling & refrigeration)
makes 8

tips You can also make the pastry using a food processor. Process flour and butter until crumbly; with motor operating, add the water and process until ingredients just come together. Or you can use ready-made shortcrust pastry.
As the meringue sets quickly, keep beating it until ready to pipe (or spread it with a metal spatula). If you don't have a blowtorch (available from kitchenware and hardware stores) you can brown the meringue very quickly under a preheated grill (broiler). Candy thermometers are available from kitchenware stores. Digital thermometers are easiest to read.

vanilla and raspberry crème brûlée tarts

185g (6 ounces) cold butter

1⅔ cups (250g) plain (all-purpose) flour

¼ cup (60ml) iced water, approximately

2 tablespoons raspberry jam (conserve)

1 vanilla bean

1 cup (250ml) milk

2 egg yolks

1 tablespoon caster (superfine) sugar

1 tablespoon cornflour (cornstarch)

½ cup (110g) caster (superfine) sugar, extra

1 Chop cold butter. Sift flour into large bowl; rub in butter until crumbly. Mix in enough of the water to make ingredients just come together. Knead dough lightly on floured surface until smooth. Flatten pastry slightly, wrap in plastic wrap; refrigerate 30 minutes.

2 Grease eight 8cm (3¼-inch) round loose-based fluted flan pans. Divide pastry into eight equal portions. Roll out each portion on floured surface or between sheets of baking paper until large enough to line pans.

3 Lift pastry into pans; press over bases and sides, trim excess pastry. Prick bases all over with fork, place pans on oven tray; refrigerate 30 minutes.

4 Preheat oven to 200°C/400°F.

5 Line pastry with baking paper; fill with dried beans or rice. Bake 15 minutes; remove paper and beans. Bake a further 10 minutes or until browned lightly and crisp. Cool. Drop 1 teaspoon of jam into each tart shell.

6 Split vanilla bean lengthways; scrape seeds into medium saucepan, add bean and milk. Bring to the boil; remove from heat. Whisk egg yolks, sugar and cornflour in medium heatproof bowl until combined; gradually whisk in hot milk mixture. Strain into same saucepan; discard vanilla bean. Whisk over high heat until mixture boils and thickens. Remove from heat; spoon into tart shells. Cool 5 minutes; refrigerate until cold.

7 Sprinkle custard with extra sugar. Using a blowtorch, caramelise sugar. Stand 5 minutes or until caramel cools and sets.

prep + cook time 1¼ hours (+ refrigeration & cooling)
makes 8

tips You can also make the pastry using a food processor. Process flour and butter until crumbly; with motor operating, add the water and process until ingredients just come together. Or you can use ready-made shortcrust pastry.
If you don't have a blowtorch (available from kitchenware and hardware stores), then place the remaining sugar and 2 tablespoons of water in a small heavy-based saucepan over medium heat; cook, stirring, for 2 minutes, until sugar dissolves. Bring to the boil. Cook, without stirring, for 5 minutes, until syrup turns deep golden. Remove from heat. Pour over cold custards and stand for 1 minute until caramel sets.

mixed berry and ricotta tart

185g (6 ounces) cold butter

1⅓ cups (200g) plain (all-purpose) flour

¼ cup (60ml) iced water, approximately

500g (1 pound) soft ricotta cheese

⅓ cup (80ml) pouring cream

⅓ cup (75g) caster (superfine) sugar

3 eggs

1 tablespoon finely grated lemon rind

200g (6½ ounces) strawberries

125g (4 ounces) blueberries

125g (4 ounces) raspberries

1 teaspoon icing (confectioner's) sugar

1 Chop cold butter. Sift flour into large bowl; rub in butter until crumbly. Mix in enough of the water to make ingredients just come together. Knead dough lightly on floured surface until smooth. Flatten pastry slightly, wrap in plastic wrap; refrigerate 30 minutes.

2 Grease 22cm (9-inch) round loose-based fluted flan pan. Roll out pastry on floured surface or between sheets of baking paper until large enough to line pan.

3 Lift pastry into pan; press over base and side, trim excess pastry. Prick base all over with fork; refrigerate 30 minutes.

4 Preheat oven to 200°C/400°F.

5 Place flan pan on oven tray, line pastry with baking paper; fill with dried beans or rice. Bake 15 minutes; remove paper and beans. Bake a further 10 minutes or until browned lightly and crisp. Remove from oven; cool.

6 Reduce oven temperature to 180°C/350°F.

7 Meanwhile, beat ricotta, cream, sugar, eggs and rind in small bowl with electric mixer until smooth.

8 Pour ricotta mixture into tart shell; bake about 35 minutes or until filling is just set. Refrigerate until cold.

9 Trim strawberries; halve if large. Top tart with berries just before serving; dust with sifted icing sugar.

prep + cook time 1½ hours (+ refrigeration) **serves** 10

tips You can also make the pastry using a food processor. Process flour and butter until crumbly; with motor operating, add the water and process until ingredients just come together. Or you can use ready-made shortcrust pastry.

apple and pear tarte tatin

100g (3 ounces) cold butter

1⅓ cups (200g) plain (all-purpose) flour

¾ cup (165g) caster (superfine) sugar

1 egg

¼ cup (60ml) water

3 small firm apples (100g)

3 small firm pears (300g)

30g (1 ounce) butter, extra

1 Chop cold butter. Sift flour and 1 tablespoon of the sugar into large bowl; rub in butter until crumbly. Add lightly beaten egg, mix until ingredients just come together. Knead dough lightly on floured surface until smooth. Roll pastry out to 22cm (9-inch) round, place on baking-paper-lined tray, cover with plastic wrap; refrigerate 30 minutes.

2 Preheat oven to 200°C/400°F.
3 Meanwhile, combine remaining sugar and the water in shallow heavy-based 20cm (8-inch) ovenproof frying pan; stir over high heat, without boiling, until sugar dissolves. Bring to the boil; boil, uncovered, without stirring, until caramel in colour.
4 Meanwhile, peel, quarter and core fruit. Add extra butter to pan; alternate apple and pear quarters, rounded-side down, in pan; cook over low heat until fruit is just tender. Remove from heat.
5 Carefully lift pastry over hot fruit mixture, gently push pastry down side of pan. Bake about 35 minutes or until pastry is browned lightly. Stand tarte in pan 10 minutes; carefully invert onto heatproof serving plate.
6 Serve immediately with double (thick) cream or ice-cream.

prep + cook time 1½ hours (+ refrigeration) **serves** 8

tips You can also make the pastry using a food processor. Process flour and butter until crumbly; with motor operating, add the water and process until ingredients just come together. Or you can use ready-made shortcrust pastry.
We used small (lunch-box size) pink lady apples and corella pears in this recipe.

apricot and pistachio tart

850g (1¾ pounds) canned
apricot halves in natural juice

2 sheets puff pastry

⅓ cup (45g) unsalted shelled
pistachios

2 tablespoons demerara sugar

2 tablespoons apricot jam
(conserve)

2 teaspoons hot water

1 Preheat oven to 240°C/475°F.
Line two oven trays with baking
paper.
2 Drain apricots; discard juice.
Dry apricots well on absorbent
paper towel; cut into wedges.

3 Halve each pastry sheet; place
halves on trays. Gently mark a 1cm
(½ inch) border around all edges,
without cutting all the way through
(this helps the edges to puff up);
prick all over, except along the
border edges, with a fork.
4 Process nuts until coarsely
chopped; reserve half. Process
remaining nuts until fine.
5 Sprinkle finely ground nuts
and half the sugar over pastry,
except the border. Top with
apricots; sprinkle with remaining
sugar and reserved nuts.
6 Bake tarts about 15 minutes or
until pastry is puffed and browned

lightly. Combine jam and the
water in small bowl; brush glaze
over apricots and pastry edges.
Bake about 2 minutes or until
browned. Serve warm tarts with
vanilla ice-cream or pouring
cream, if you like.

prep + cook time 40 minutes
serves 8

tip If in season, use halved
and seeded fresh apricots.

caramelised apple and custard tarts

185g (6 ounces) cold butter

1⅔ cups (250g) plain (all-purpose) flour

¼ cup (60ml) iced water, approximately

4 small apples (400g)

2 tablespoons raw sugar

frangipane

50g (1½ ounces) butter

¼ cup (55g) caster (superfine) sugar

1 egg

½ cup (60g) ground almonds

2 tablespoons plain (all-purpose) flour

vanilla pastry cream

½ vanilla bean

1 cup (250ml) milk

2 egg yolks

¼ cup (55g) caster (superfine) sugar

2 tablespoons cornflour (cornstarch)

1 Have butter for almond frangipane at room temperature.
2 Chop cold butter. Sift flour into large bowl; rub in butter until crumbly. Mix in enough of the water to make ingredients just come together. Knead dough lightly on floured surface until smooth. Flatten pastry slightly, wrap in plastic wrap; refrigerate 30 minutes.
3 Grease eight 8cm (3¼-inch) round loose-based fluted flan pans. Divide pastry into eight equal portions. Roll out each portion on floured surface or between sheets of baking paper until large enough to line pans.
4 Lift pastry into pans; press over bases and sides, trim excess pastry. Prick bases all over with fork, place pans on oven tray; refrigerate 30 minutes.
5 Make frangipane and vanilla pastry cream.
6 Preheat oven to 200°C/400°F.
7 Line pastry with baking paper; fill with dried beans or rice. Bake 15 minutes; remove paper and beans. Bake a further 10 minutes or until browned lightly and crisp.
8 Spread pastry cream into tart shells; top with frangipane.
9 Halve and core apples. Use mandoline or V-slicer to slice one apple half thinly. Cut slices in half lengthways; arrange on top of frangipane, sprinkle with sugar. Repeat with remaining apple. Bake about 30 minutes or until browned lightly.

FRANGIPANE Whisk butter and sugar in medium bowl until light and fluffy; whisk in egg, until combined. Stir in ground almonds and sifted flour.

VANILLA PASTRY CREAM Split vanilla bean, scrape seeds into medium saucepan, add bean and milk. Bring to the boil; remove from heat. Whisk egg yolks, sugar and cornflour in medium heatproof bowl until combined; gradually whisk in hot milk mixture. Strain into same pan; discard vanilla bean. Whisk over high heat until mixture boils and thickens. Remove from heat; cover surface with plastic wrap.

prep + cook time 1¼ hours (+ refrigeration) **makes** 8

tips We used very small pink lady apples, the ones suitable for kids' lunchboxes.
You can also make the pastry using a food processor. Process flour and butter until crumbly; with motor operating, add the water and process until ingredients just come together. Or you can use ready-made shortcrust pastry.

brandied apricot and prune tart

1 cup (150g) coarsely chopped dried apricots

1 cup (180g) coarsely chopped seeded prunes

¼ cup (60ml) brandy

155g (5 ounces) cold butter

1⅔ cups (250g) plain (all-purpose) flour

¼ cup (60ml) iced water, approximately

½ teaspoon mixed spice

¼ cup (55g) firmly packed light brown sugar

½ cup (125ml) water, extra

2 tablespoons cornflour (cornstarch)

1 egg white

1 tablespoon raw sugar

1 Combine fruit and brandy in medium bowl; stand 10 minutes.
2 Chop cold butter. Sift flour into large bowl; rub in butter until crumbly. Mix in enough of the water to make ingredients just come together. Knead dough lightly on floured surface until smooth. Flatten pastry slightly, wrap in plastic wrap; refrigerate 30 minutes.
3 Meanwhile, combine fruit mixture, spice, brown sugar and the extra water in medium saucepan; cook, covered, over medium heat, about 5 minutes or until sugar dissolves and fruit is soft. Blend cornflour with 1 tablespoon water in small bowl, stir into fruit mixture; cook, stirring, until mixture boils and thickens. Cool.
4 Grease 24cm (9½-inch) round loose-based fluted flan pan. Roll out three-quarters of the pastry on floured surface or between sheets of baking paper until large enough to line pan.
5 Lift pastry into pan; press over base and side, trim excess pastry. Prick base all over with fork, place on oven tray; refrigerate 30 minutes.
6 Preheat oven to 200°C/400°F.

7 Roll out remaining pastry until 5mm (¼-inch) thick; cut pastry into 1cm (½-inch) wide strips.
8 Spread fruit mixture into tart shell. Arrange pastry strips in lattice pattern over fruit mixture, extending strips over edge of pan; press edges to seal, trim excess pastry. Brush pastry with egg white; sprinkle with raw sugar.
9 Bake tart about 45 minutes or until browned lightly; stand tart in pan 10 minutes, before serving with custard or vanilla ice-cream, if you like.

prep + cook time 1½ hours (+ standing & refrigeration) **serves** 10

tips You can also make the pastry using a food processor. Process flour and butter until crumbly; with motor operating, add the water and process until ingredients just come together. Or you can use ready-made shortcrust pastry.

coffee custard tarts

185g (6 ounces) cold butter

1⅔ cups (250g) plain (all-purpose) flour

¼ cup (60ml) iced water, approximately

1¼ cups (310ml) milk

1½ tablespoons instant coffee granules

3 egg yolks

2 tablespoons caster (superfine) sugar

1 tablespoon cornflour (cornstarch)

125g (4 ounces) dark eating (semi-sweet) chocolate

2 teaspoons vegetable oil

edible gold leaf

1 Chop cold butter. Sift flour into large bowl; rub in butter until crumbly. Mix in enough of the water to make ingredients just come together. Knead dough lightly on floured surface until smooth. Flatten pastry slightly, wrap in plastic wrap; refrigerate 30 minutes.

2 Grease eight 8cm (3¼-inch) round loose-based fluted flan pans. Divide pastry into eight equal portions. Roll out each portion on floured surface or between sheets of baking paper until large enough to line pans.

3 Lift pastry into pans; press over bases and sides, trim excess pastry. Prick bases all over with fork, place pans on oven tray; refrigerate 30 minutes.

4 Preheat oven to 200°C/400°F.

5 Line pastry with baking paper; fill with dried beans or rice. Bake, on oven tray, 15 minutes; remove paper and beans. Bake a further 10 minutes or until browned lightly and crisp.

6 Meanwhile, combine milk and coffee in medium saucepan; bring to the boil, remove from heat.

7 Whisk egg yolks, sugar and cornflour in medium heatproof bowl until combined; gradually whisk in hot milk mixture. Strain into same pan. Whisk over high heat until mixture boils and thickens. Remove from heat; spoon into tart shells. Refrigerate until cold.

8 Break chocolate into small heatproof bowl; add oil. Place bowl over small saucepan of simmering water (don't let water touch base of bowl); stir until chocolate mixture is smooth. Pour chocolate mixture over cold tarts. Stand at room temperature until set. Decorate with gold leaf just before serving.

prep + cook time 1¼ hours (+ refrigeration & standing)
makes 8

tips You can also make the pastry using a food processor. Process flour and butter until crumbly; with motor operating, add the water and process until ingredients just come together. Or you can use ready-made shortcrust pastry.
Edible gold leaf is available at specialty food shops. Use tweezers (not your fingers, as it will stick) to position it just before serving.

puddings

sticky toffee date puddings

90g (3 ounces) butter

2 eggs

250g (8 ounces) seeded dried dates

1¼ cups (310ml) water

1 teaspoon bicarbonate of soda (baking soda)

¾ cup (165g) caster (superfine) sugar

2 teaspoons vanilla extract

1¼ cups (185g) plain (all-purpose) flour

toffee sauce

1 cup (220g) caster (superfine) sugar

1¼ cups (310ml) pouring cream (see notes)

1 Have butter and eggs at room temperature.
2 Preheat oven to 180°C/350°F. Grease 8-hole (½-cup/125ml) mini fluted tube pan.
3 Using scissors, coarsely cut dates into medium saucepan; add the water. Bring to the boil; remove from heat, stir in soda. Cool.
4 Beat butter, eggs, sugar and extract in small bowl with electric mixer until light and fluffy. Stir in sifted flour and date mixture. Divide mixture into pan holes. Bake about 15 minutes.
5 Meanwhile, make toffee sauce.
6 Serve warm puddings with toffee sauce and a little extra pouring cream, if you like.

TOFFEE SAUCE Cook sugar in medium frying pan, over medium heat, without stirring, until sugar melts and turns a dark caramel colour. Gently add the cream (be careful, as it will splatter); stir to combine. Simmer sauce, uncovered, about 1 minute or until thickened slightly.

prep + cook time 35 minutes
makes 8

notes It is fine to use just the one 300ml carton of cream for this recipe.
Swirl, don't stir, the toffee; this will encourage uniform melting and colouring of the sugar.

caramel pear bread puddings

3 medium pears (690g)

⅓ cup (75g) firmly packed light brown sugar

90g (3 ounces) butter

2 tablespoons finely grated lemon rind

60g (2 ounces) butter, extra

21 slices white bread (945g)

¼ cup (55g) caster (superfine) sugar

2 teaspoons ground cinnamon

pear wafers

2 corella pears (200g)

½ cup (110g) caster (superfine) sugar

1 Preheat oven 200°C/400°F. Grease six ¾-cup (180ml) ovenproof dishes.
2 Make pear wafers.
3 Peel, core and coarsely chop pears.
4 Combine brown sugar, butter and rind in medium saucepan; stir over high heat, without boiling, until sugar dissolves. Add chopped pear; simmer, covered, about 5 minutes or until pear is tender. Remove from heat.
5 Meanwhile, melt extra butter. Remove crusts from bread. Using 5cm (2-inch) round cutter, cut rounds from 6 slices of bread; using 6.5cm (2¾-inch) round cutter, cut rounds from 6 slices of bread. Cut each of the remaining 9 slices of bread into 3 finger lengths. Brush all bread pieces, both sides, with melted butter. Sprinkle one side of bread pieces with combined caster sugar and cinnamon.
6 Place smaller bread rounds, sugar-side down, into base of moulds. Line side of each mould with fingers of bread, sugar-side out, overlapping slightly.
7 Divide pear mixture evenly into moulds, reserving any leftover caramel sauce. Place larger bread rounds, sugar-side up, on top of pear mixture.
8 Bake puddings for about 25 minutes or until browned lightly and crisp. Serve puddings with pear wafers, leftover caramel sauce, and pouring cream or ice-cream, if you like.

PEAR WAFERS Line oven tray with baking paper. Using a mandoline or V-slicer, thinly slice pears lengthways. Place pear slices, in single layer, on tray; sprinkle with sugar. Bake about 20 minutes or until pears are crisp. Stand the tray on a wire rack to cool.

prep + cook time 50 minutes
makes 6

tip We used dariole moulds for the pudding; a texas muffin pan would work well, too.

mocha raisin pudding

90g (3 ounces) butter

2 eggs

1 cup (150g) raisins

1 teaspoon bicarbonate of soda (baking soda)

2 teaspoons instant coffee granules

⅔ cup (180ml) boiling water

200g (6½ ounces) dark eating (semi-sweet) chocolate

½ cup (110g) firmly packed light brown sugar

2 teaspoons vanilla extract

1 cup (150g) plain (all-purpose) flour

½ cup (75g) self-raising flour

⅓ cup (80ml) milk

mocha sauce

100g (3 ounces) dark eating (semi-sweet) chocolate

½ cup (110g) firmly packed light brown sugar

60g (2 ounces) butter

1¼ cups (310ml) pouring cream (see note)

1 teaspoon instant coffee granules

boozy muscatels

½ cup (110g) caster (superfine) sugar

½ cup (125ml) water

2 tablespoons bourbon or whisky

250g (8 ounces) small bunches dried muscatels

1 Have butter and eggs at room temperature.

2 Preheat oven to 180°C/350°F. Grease six 1-cup (250ml) pudding bowls well.

3 Combine raisins, soda, coffee and the boiling water in medium heatproof bowl; stand 15 minutes.

4 Chop chocolate coarsely.

5 Beat butter, eggs, sugar and extract in small bowl with electric mixer until light and fluffy (mixture will curdle at this stage, but will come together later); transfer mixture to large bowl. Stir in sifted flours, milk, chocolate and raisin mixture. Spoon mixture into pudding bowls.

6 Place puddings in large baking dish; pour in enough boiling water to come halfway up sides of bowls. Lay a piece of baking paper, then a sheet of foil over the top of the dishes. Bake about 20 minutes.

7 Meanwhile, make mocha sauce and boozy muscatels.

8 Remove puddings from baking dish; stand in bowls 5 minutes before turning onto serving plates. Serve warm puddings with sauce and muscatels.

MOCHA SAUCE Break chocolate into medium saucepan; add sugar, butter, cream and coffee. Stir over heat until smooth.

BOOZY MUSCATELS Combine sugar, the water and bourbon in medium saucepan; stir over high heat, without boiling, until sugar dissolves. Bring to the boil. Reduce heat; simmer, uncovered, 3 minutes. Add muscatels; simmer, uncovered, 2 minutes.

prep + cook time 45 minutes (+ standing) **serves** 6

note It is fine to use just the one 300ml carton of cream for the mocha sauce.

rose queen puddings

4 eggs

4 slices white bread (180g)

2 cups (500ml) milk

2 teaspoons cornflour (cornstarch)

1¼ cups (275g) caster (superfine) sugar

1 teaspoon rosewater

⅓ cup (110g) rose petal jam

2 tablespoons caster (superfine) sugar, extra

pink food colouring

organic pink rose petals

1 Have eggs at room temperature; separate eggs.
2 Remove crusts from bread; chop bread finely. Place bread in medium heatproof bowl.
3 Bring milk to the boil in small saucepan; pour over bread, stand 15 minutes.
4 Preheat oven to 160°C/325°F.
5 Whisk egg yolks, cornflour, ¼ cup of the sugar and the rosewater in medium bowl until combined. Stir in warm milk and bread mixture.
6 Pour mixture into six 1-cup (250ml) ovenproof dishes, place on oven tray. Bake puddings about 25 minutes or until custard is set; remove from oven. Spoon jam equally over custards.

7 Increase oven temperature to 200°C/400°F.
8 Beat egg whites with remaining sugar in small bowl with electric mixer until sugar is dissolved. Spread meringue over jam. Bake puddings about 3 minutes or until meringue is browned lightly.
9 Combine extra sugar and a few drops of food colouring in small resealable bag; rub bag until sugar is coloured evenly. Serve puddings sprinkled with pink sugar and rose petals.

prep + cook time 50 minutes (+ standing) **serves** 6

notes Rose petal jam is available from Middle-Eastern food stores and delis, use a berry jam if you prefer. Organic flower petals are available from some florists; make sure they have not been sprayed with chemicals.

apple almond cobbler

3 medium green-skinned apples (450g)

½ cup (80g) sultanas

½ cup (125ml) pure maple syrup

30g (1 ounce) butter

1 cup (150g) self-raising flour

2 tablespoons light brown sugar

30g (1 ounce) butter, extra

½ cup (125ml) pouring cream

¾ cup (60g) flaked almonds

1 Preheat oven to 180°C/350°F. Grease 1.5-litre (6-cup) ovenproof dish well.

2 Peel, core and halve apples. Place apples, cut-side up, in single layer, in dish, sprinkle with sultanas; drizzle with maple syrup, dot apples with butter. Cover dish with foil; bake 20 minutes.

3 Sift flour and sugar into medium bowl; rub in extra butter. Add cream; use a knife to cut the cream through the flour mixture to make a soft sticky dough.

4 Remove foil from dish; spoon dough evenly over apple halves, sprinkle with nuts. Bake a further 25 minutes or until apples are tender and cobbler is browned lightly. Stand 10 minutes before serving with cream, custard or ice-cream.

prep + cook time 1 hour
serves 6

warm strawberry rhubarb crumbles

1 bunch rhubarb (500g)

250g (8 ounces) strawberries

¼ cup (55g) caster (superfine) sugar

2 teaspoons vanilla extract

2 eggs

¼ cup (55g) caster (superfine) sugar, extra

1 tablespoon cornflour (cornstarch)

1¼ cups (310ml) pouring cream (see note)

1 cup (250ml) milk

2 teaspoons vanilla extract, extra

crumble

60g (2 ounces) cold butter

½ cup (75g) self-raising flour

¼ cup (55g) demerara sugar

½ cup (60g) coarsely chopped pecans

1 Preheat oven to 180°C/350°F.
2 Trim rhubarb and chop into 5cm (2-inch) pieces. Hull strawberries. Combine rhubarb, strawberries, sugar and extract in shallow baking dish. Bake, uncovered, 20 minutes or until rhubarb softens.
3 Meanwhile, make crumble.
4 Whisk eggs, extra sugar and cornflour in medium saucepan until combined; gradually whisk in cream and milk. Cook, whisking, until mixture boils and thickens. Remove from heat; stir in extra extract.
5 Pour custard into six heatproof serving glasses. Top with rhubarb mixture, then crumble.

CRUMBLE Line oven tray with baking paper. Chop butter finely. Combine sifted flour and sugar in medium bowl; rub in butter until crumbly, stir in nuts. Spoon mixture in a thin layer onto tray. Bake about 15 minutes or until mixture is browned lightly. Cool 10 minutes before crumbling mixture coarsely.

prep + cook time 45 minutes
serves 6

note It is fine to use just the one 300ml carton of cream for this recipe.

chocolate honeycomb self-saucing pudding

90g (3 ounces) butter

200g (6½ ounces) chocolate-coated honeycomb

1 cup (150g) self-raising flour

2 tablespoons cocoa powder

½ cup (110g) firmly packed light brown sugar

½ cup (125ml) milk

1¼ cups (310ml) water

¾ cup (165g) firmly packed light brown sugar, extra

2 tablespoons cocoa powder, extra

1¼ cups (310ml) thickened (heavy) cream (see note)

1 Preheat oven to 180°C/350°F. Grease 1.5-litre (6-cup) or six 1-cup (250ml) individual ovenproof dishes well.

2 Melt butter; cool. Chop honeycomb finely. Sift flour, cocoa and sugar into large bowl. Stir in butter, milk and half the honeycomb. Spread mixture into dish.

3 Boil the water. Sift extra sugar and cocoa over top of pudding. Carefully pour boiling water over top of sugar mixture. Bake pudding about 40 minutes.

4 Meanwhile, beat cream in small bowl with electric mixer until soft peaks form.

5 Serve pudding with cream; sprinkle with the remaining chopped honeycomb.

prep + cook time 50 minutes
serves 6

notes It is fine to use just one 300ml carton of cream for this recipe.
Individual puddings will take about 30 minutes to cook.

apple sponge puddings

4 medium green-skinned apples (600g)

¼ cup (55g) caster (superfine) sugar

¼ cup (60ml) water

1 cinnamon stick

2 eggs

1 teaspoon vanilla extract

1 tablespoon finely grated lemon rind

¼ cup (55g) caster (superfine) sugar, extra

½ cup (75g) self-raising flour

⅓ cup (25g) shredded coconut

2 teaspoons icing (confectioners') sugar

1 Preheat oven to 180°C/350°F. Grease four 1-cup (250ml) ovenproof dishes.

2 Peel, quarter and core apples. Combine apples, sugar, the water and cinnamon in medium saucepan; cook, covered, about 8 minutes or until apples are tender. Discard cinnamon. Spoon apple into dishes.

3 Beat eggs, extract, rind and extra sugar in small bowl with electric mixer until thick and creamy. Transfer to medium bowl; fold in sifted flour and coconut. Spoon sponge mixture over apple. Place dishes on oven tray.

4 Bake puddings about 15 minutes or until browned lightly. Stand 5 minutes before serving dusted with sifted icing sugar; accompany with ice-cream, if you like.

prep + cook time 40 minutes
makes 4

cranberry and orange hazelnut steamed puddings

125g (4 ounces) butter

3 eggs

1⅓ cups (175g) dried cranberries

¾ cup (240g) whole cranberry sauce

⅔ cup (150g) caster (superfine) sugar

1 teaspoon vanilla extract

1 tablespoon finely grated orange rind

1½ cups (225g) self-raising flour

½ cup (60g) ground hazelnuts

⅓ cup (80ml) orange juice

½ cup (125ml) water

2 tablespoons caster (superfine) sugar, extra

1 Have butter and eggs at room temperature.

2 Preheat oven to 180°C/350°F. Grease six ½-cup (125ml) pudding bowls well.

3 Combine cranberries and sauce in medium saucepan; stir over low heat until sauce is melted. Simmer, uncovered, 3 minutes. Cool. Spoon 1 tablespoon of cranberry mixture into each pudding bowl. Reserve remaining cranberry mixture.

4 Beat butter, eggs, sugar, extract and rind in small bowl with electric mixer until light and fluffy (mixture will curdle at this stage, but will come together later). Transfer mixture to large bowl; stir in sifted flour, ground hazelnuts and juice, in two batches. Divide mixture into pudding bowls.

5 Place puddings in large baking dish; pour in enough boiling water to come halfway up sides of bowls. Lay a piece of baking paper, then a sheet of foil over the top of the dishes. Bake about 20 minutes.

6 Reheat reserved cranberry mixture in small saucepan with the water and extra sugar. Simmer about 5 minutes or until mixture is slightly thickened. Strain sauce; discard solids.

7 Remove puddings from baking dish; stand in bowls 5 minutes before turning onto serving plates. Drizzle with cranberry sauce; serve with pouring cream or custard.

prep + cook time 45 minutes (+ cooling & standing) **makes** 6

dessert cakes

pistachio almond cake with pomegranate sauce

2 cups (560g) greek-style yogurt

1 cup (160g) almond kernels

1 cup (140g) unsalted shelled pistachios

4 eggs

40g (1½ ounces) butter

¾ cup (165g) caster (superfine) sugar

1 cup (120g) ground almonds

1 cup (160g) icing (confectioners') sugar

1 medium pomegranate (320g)

pomegranate sauce

2 medium pomegranates (620g)

¼ cup (55g) caster (superfine) sugar

1 tablespoon cornflour (cornstarch)

1 Place yogurt in a fine strainer lined with muslin or absorbent paper; place over jug or bowl. Cover; refrigerate overnight.

2 Preheat oven to 160°C/325°F. Grease deep 25cm (10-inch) round cake pan; line base with baking paper.

3 Spread almonds, in single layer, on oven tray; roast, uncovered, 10 minutes. Add pistachios; roast another 2 minutes. Remove nuts from tray; cool. Process nuts until coarsely ground.

4 Separate eggs. Melt butter.

5 Beat egg whites and caster sugar in small bowl with electric mixer until sugar dissolves. Beat in egg yolks. Transfer mixture to large bowl; stir in nuts, ground almonds and butter.

6 Spread mixture into pan. Bake cake about 45 minutes. Cool cake in pan.

7 Meanwhile, make pomegranate sauce.

8 Whisk drained yogurt and sifted icing sugar in medium bowl until soft peaks form.

9 Halve pomegranate; remove seeds. Serve cake with yogurt mixture, seeds and sauce.

POMEGRANATE SAUCE Cut pomegranates in half, squeeze on citrus juicer. You need 1 cup juice. Combine sugar and cornflour in small saucepan, gradually stir in juice. Cook, stirring, over high heat until mixture boils and thickens.

prep + cook time 1½ hours (+ refrigeration & cooling)
serves 12

apple and cinnamon crunch cake with cinnamon anglaise

185g (6 ounces) butter

3 eggs

8 small red-skinned apples (800g)

1.5 litres (6 cups) water

2 cups (440g) caster (superfine) sugar

1 cinnamon stick

2 teaspoons vanilla extract

1 cup (220g) caster (superfine) sugar, extra

1 cup (120g) ground almonds

1½ cups (225g) self-raising flour

½ cup (125ml) buttermilk

cinnamon crunch topping

30g (1 ounce) butter

2 tablespoons light brown sugar

2 tablespoons plain (all-purpose) flour

1 teaspoon ground cinnamon

cinnamon anglaise

¾ cup (180ml) pouring cream

1⅓ cups (330ml) milk

1 cinnamon stick

4 egg yolks

¼ cup (55g) caster (superfine) sugar

1 Have butter and eggs at room temperature.

2 Peel apples, leaving stems intact.

3 Combine the water, sugar and cinnamon in a saucepan large enough to hold apples in a single layer; stir over high heat, without boiling until sugar dissolves. Bring to the boil, add apples; cover apples with a round of baking paper and a heatproof plate to keep apples submerged in syrup. Return to the boil. Reduce heat; simmer, covered, about 8 minutes or until apples are tender. Remove apples from pan with a slotted spoon. Cool 10 minutes.

4 Preheat oven to 160°C/325°F. Grease 26cm (10½-inch) closed springform pan; insert base of pan upside down to make cake easier to remove. Line base with baking paper.

5 Beat butter, extract and extra sugar in small bowl with electric mixer until light and fluffy. Beat in eggs, one at a time. Transfer mixture to large bowl. Stir in ground almonds, sifted flour and buttermilk, in two batches. Spread mixture into pan. Place apples, evenly spaced, around outside edge of pan, pushing apples down to base of pan.

6 Bake cake 30 minutes.

7 Meanwhile, make cinnamon crunch topping. Crumble topping over cake. Bake cake a further 45 minutes. Stand cake in pan 15 minutes.

8 Make cinnamon anglaise. Serve warm cake with anglaise.

CINNAMON CRUNCH TOPPING
Melt butter in small saucepan; stir in remaining ingredients. Refrigerate 15 minutes.

CINNAMON ANGLAISE
Combine cream, milk and cinnamon in medium saucepan; bring to the boil. Remove from heat, cover; stand 20 minutes. Whisk egg yolks and sugar in medium bowl until creamy. Gradually whisk in warm milk mixture. Return mixture to pan; stir over medium-high heat, without boiling, until custard thickens and coats the back of a spoon. Strain into medium jug; discard cinnamon stick.

prep + cook time 2 hours (+ refrigeration & standing)
serves 8

notes We used very small pink lady apples, the ones suitable for kids' lunchboxes.
If you prefer, stir the anglaise in a heatproof bowl over a saucepan of simmering water to prevent the custard curdling. The anglaise can be served either warm or cooled.

lemon curd meringue cake with blueberries

4 egg whites

1 cup (150g) almond kernels

1 cup (220g) caster (superfine) sugar

125g (4 ounces) white eating chocolate

1¼ cups (310ml) double (thick) cream (see notes)

125g (4 ounces) fresh blueberries

lemon curd

250g (8 ounces) cold butter

2 eggs

⅔ cup (160ml) lemon juice

1⅓ cups (300g) caster (superfine) sugar

2 egg yolks

1 Have egg whites at room temperature.

2 Make lemon curd.

3 Preheat oven to 160°C/325°F. Grease 24cm (9½-inch) closed springform pan; insert base of pan upside down to make cake easier to remove. Line base with baking paper.

4 Spread nuts, in a single layer, on oven tray; roast, uncovered, about 12 minutes or until skins begin to split. Cool. Chop nuts finely.

5 Beat egg whites and ¼ cup of the sugar in small bowl with electric mixer until firm peaks form. Add remaining sugar; beat on high speed about 5 minutes or until sugar is dissolved.

6 Meanwhile, coarsely grate chocolate; fold into meringue mixture with nuts. Spread mixture into pan. Bake about 40 minutes. Cool meringue in pan.

7 Beat cream in small bowl with electric mixer until soft peaks form; fold in curd.

8 Spoon curd mixture onto meringue. Refrigerate several hours or overnight until firm.

9 Top cake with blueberries (see notes on how to make toffee blueberries) just before serving.

LEMON CURD Chop butter; place in medium saucepan. Lightly beat eggs in small bowl; strain into pan. Add remaining ingredients; stir over low heat, without boiling, about 10 minutes or until mixture thickly coats the back of a wooden spoon. Transfer curd to medium heatproof bowl. Cover; refrigerate until cold.

prep + cook time 1¾ hours (+ refrigeration, cooling & standing) **serves** 12

notes It is fine to use just the one 300ml carton of cream for this recipe.
To make the toffee-dipped blueberries used to decorate the cake: Stir 1 cup white sugar with ½ cup water over medium heat until sugar is dissolved. Bring to the boil; boil, without stirring, until sugar has thickened and turns a caramel colour. Push a wooden toothpick into each blueberry. Remove toffee from heat; allow bubbles to subside. Working with one blueberry at a time, hold berry by the toothpick, dip into the thickened toffee. Hold blueberry above the toffee so that a trail of toffee falls from the berry. Hold upside down until starting to set, then place onto cake. You may need to reheat the toffee if it starts to thicken too much.

honey muscat cake with orange syrup

250g (8 ounces) butter

3 eggs

½ cup (110g) caster (superfine) sugar

½ cup (175g) honey

2 cups (150g) self-raising flour

½ cup (125ml) muscat

½ cup (140g) greek-style yogurt

¾ cup (200g) greek-style yogurt, extra

orange syrup

⅔ cup (160ml) orange juice

½ cup (125ml) water

¾ cup (165g) caster (superfine) sugar

1 tablespoon muscat

1 Have butter and eggs at room temperature.
2 Preheat oven to 180°C/350°F. Grease 24cm (9½-inch) bundt pan well; sprinkle with a little flour, tap out excess flour.
3 Beat butter and sugar in small bowl with electric mixer until light and fluffy. Beat in honey, then eggs, one at a time. Transfer mixture to large bowl. Stir in sifted flour, muscat and yogurt in two batches. Spread mixture into pan.
4 Bake cake about 45 minutes. Turn cake onto wire rack over shallow tray.
5 Meanwhile, make orange syrup. Reserve ⅔ cup syrup. Pour the remaining hot syrup over hot cake.
6 Serve cake warm, topped with some extra yogurt; drizzle with reserved syrup.

ORANGE SYRUP Combine ingredients in small saucepan; stir over high heat, without boiling, until sugar dissolves. Bring to the boil; remove from heat.

prep + cook time 1¼ hours
serves 10

notes Muscat is a sweet dessert wine available from most liquor stores. We used tiny fresh grapes to decorate the cake; dried muscatels would also be good.

blood orange syrup cakes with orange cream

You will need about 10 blood oranges for this recipe.

125g (4 ounces) butter

2 eggs

2 teaspoons finely grated blood orange rind

½ cup (110g) caster (superfine) sugar

1 cup (150g) self-raising flour

⅓ cup (80ml) blood orange juice

2 medium blood oranges (320g)

1 cup (250ml) double (thick) cream

blood orange syrup

1 medium blood orange (160g)

1 cup (250ml) blood orange juice

1 cup (220g) caster (superfine) sugar

¾ cup (180ml) water

1 tablespoon lemon juice

1 Have butter and eggs at room temperature; separate eggs.
2 Preheat oven to 180°C/350°F. Grease eight ½-cup (125ml) oval friand pans well.
3 Beat butter, rind and sugar in small bowl with electric mixer until light and fluffy. Beat in egg yolks, one at a time. Transfer to medium bowl; stir in sifted flour and juice, in two batches.
4 Beat egg whites in clean small bowl with electric mixer until soft peaks form; fold into cake batter, in two batches.
5 Divide mixture evenly into pans; bake about 20 minutes. Turn cakes, top-side up, onto wire rack over shallow tray.
6 Meanwhile, peel oranges thickly to remove all white pith. Cut each orange crossways into six slices.
7 Make blood orange syrup. Reserve 1⅓ cups of the syrup; freeze ⅓ cup of the reserved syrup for 10 minutes or until cold.

8 Pour remaining hot syrup over hot cakes; reheat syrup if needed.
9 Whisk cream with the cold reserved syrup in medium bowl until soft peaks form.
10 Serve cakes with orange cream and sliced oranges, drizzle cakes with reserved reheated syrup.

BLOOD ORANGE SYRUP Using zester, peel thin strips of orange rind. Combine rind with orange juice, sugar and the water in small saucepan; stir over high heat, without boiling, until sugar dissolves. Bring to the boil; remove from heat. Stir in lemon juice.

prep + cook time 50 minutes (+ freezing) **serves** 8

layered banana butterscotch cake

You need about 7 overripe medium bananas for this recipe.

375g (12 ounces) butter

6 eggs

2 cups (440g) caster (superfine) sugar

2 cups mashed overripe bananas

3 cups (450g) self-raising flour

½ cup (75g) plain (all-purpose) flour

2 cups (240g) pecan halves

butterscotch frosting

1 cup (220g) firmly packed light brown sugar

½ cup (125ml) pouring cream

125g (4 ounces) butter

250g (8 ounces) cream cheese

butterscotch sauce

185g (6 ounces) butter

1 cup (220g) firmly packed light brown sugar

1 cup (250ml) pouring cream

1 Have the butter, cream cheese, and eggs at room temperature.
2 Preheat oven to 180°C/350°F. Grease two deep 20cm (8-inch) round cake pans; line bases with baking paper.
3 Make butterscotch frosting and butterscotch sauce.
4 Beat butter and sugar in large bowl with electric mixer until light and fluffy. Beat in eggs, one at a time. Stir in banana, then sifted flours. Divide mixture evenly between pans.
5 Bake cakes about 50 minutes. Stand cakes in pan 5 minutes before turning, top-side up, onto wire racks to cool.
6 Roast nuts, in single layer, on oven tray, about 10 minutes or until browned lightly, cool. Chop nuts coarsely.
7 Trim tops of cakes to make level. Split cakes in half. Place one cake layer, cut-side up, on serving plate; spread with ¼ cup butterscotch sauce, then ½ cup butterscotch frosting.
8 Spread cut surface of next cake layer with another ¼ cup butterscotch sauce; place, sauce-side down, on top of first layer. Spread top of cake with another ¼ cup sauce, then ½ cup frosting.
9 Repeat layering with remaining cake, finishing with frosting. Spread remaining frosting over side of cake. Press nuts onto side of cake. Refrigerate cake 2 hours or until firm.
10 Serve cake drizzled with remaining butterscotch sauce.

BUTTERSCOTCH FROSTING
Place sugar, cream and half the butter in small saucepan; cook, stirring, over medium heat until smooth. Bring to the boil, stirring constantly. Reduce heat; simmer, uncovered, 5 minutes. Transfer mixture to large heatproof bowl; refrigerate until cold. Beat remaining butter with cream cheese in medium bowl with electric mixer until combined. Gradually beat in cold butterscotch mixture. Cover; refrigerate about 1½ hours or until spreadable.

BUTTERSCOTCH SAUCE Chop butter, place in medium saucepan with sugar and cream; cook, stirring, until smooth. Bring to the boil. Reduce heat; simmer, uncovered, 3 minutes. Transfer to medium heatproof bowl. Cover; refrigerate until cold.

prep + cook time 2 hours (+ cooling & refrigeration)
serves 12

chocolate cheesecakes with caramel cream

80g (2½ ounces) butter

2 eggs

½ cup (125ml) milk

2 teaspoons white vinegar

1 teaspoon vanilla extract

⅔ cup (150g) caster (superfine) sugar

1 cup (150g) plain (all-purpose) flour

¼ cup (25g) cocoa powder

½ teaspoon bicarbonate of soda (baking soda)

topping

250g (8 ounces) cream cheese

1 egg

1 teaspoon vanilla extract

⅓ cup (75g) caster (superfine) sugar

caramel cream

60g (2 ounces) butter

½ cup (110g) firmly packed light brown sugar

1¼ cups (310ml) thickened (heavy) cream (see notes)

1 Have butter, eggs and cream cheese at room temperature.

2 Preheat oven to 180°C/350°F. Grease eight holes of a 12-hole (¾-cup/180ml) loose-based cheesecake pan.

3 Combine milk and vinegar in jug. Beat butter, eggs, extract, caster sugar, sifted dry ingredients and milk mixture in small bowl with electric mixer on low speed until ingredients are combined. Increase speed to medium; beat about 2 minutes or until mixture changes to a paler colour. Divide mixture into eight pan holes. Bake 10 minutes.

4 Meanwhile, make topping.

5 Remove cakes from oven. Divide topping between cakes, return to oven, bake a further 10 minutes or until topping is barely set; cool in pan.

6 Meanwhile, make caramel cream.

7 Serve warm cakes with caramel cream. Dust cheesecakes with a little extra sifted cocoa powder, if you like, and top with chocolate shapes just before serving. (To make chocolate shapes, see notes.)

TOPPING Beat ingredients in small bowl with electric mixer until combined.

CARAMEL CREAM Combine butter, sugar and ¼ cup of the cream in small saucepan. Stir over high heat until smooth. Bring to the boil. Reduce heat; simmer, uncovered, 3 minutes. Transfer to medium heatproof bowl; cool to room temperature. Beat remaining cream in small bowl with electric mixer until soft peaks form. Swirl caramel through cream.

prep + cook time 50 minutes (+ cooling) **makes** 8

notes It is fine to use just the one 300ml carton of cream for this recipe.

A cheesecake pan is similar to a texas muffin pan, only the base is removable.

To make chocolate shapes: Melt 50g (1½ ounces) dark chocolate; place into a resealable plastic bag. Cut a tiny snip off one corner, and pipe small shapes onto baking paper. Leave shapes to set at room temperature.

lemon berry cake with yogurt custard

250g (8 ounces) butter

3 eggs

1 tablespoon finely grated lemon rind

1½ cups (330g) caster (superfine) sugar

1½ cups (225g) self-raising flour

½ cup (75g) plain (all-purpose) flour

½ cup (140g) greek-style yogurt

⅓ cup (80ml) lemon juice

450g (14½ ounces) frozen mixed berries

yogurt custard

4 egg yolks

1¼ cups (310ml) pouring cream (see note)

½ cup (110g) caster (superfine) sugar

1 cup (280g) greek-style yogurt

1 Have butter and eggs at room temperature.

2 Preheat oven to 160°C/325°F. Grease deep 22cm (9-inch) square cake pan; line base and sides with baking paper, extending paper 5cm (2 inches) over sides.

3 Beat butter, rind and caster sugar in small bowl with electric mixer until light and fluffy. Beat in eggs, one at a time. Transfer to large bowl; stir in sifted flours, yogurt and juice, in two batches. Spread half the mixture into pan; sprinkle with half the frozen berries. Top with remaining cake batter, then remaining berries.

4 Bake cake about 1½ hours. Stand cake in pan 10 minutes before turning, top-side up, onto wire rack.

5 Meanwhile, make yogurt custard.

6 Serve cake warm with yogurt custard.

YOGURT CUSTARD Stir egg yolks, cream and sugar in small saucepan, over low heat, without boiling, until mixture thickens. Remove from heat; stir in yogurt.

prep + cook time 2 hours
serves 10

note It is fine to use just the one 300ml carton of cream for this recipe.

sticky ginger cake with grilled toffee figs

250g (8 ounces) butter

3 eggs

1 large firm pear (330g)

1½ cups (330g) caster (superfine) sugar

⅓ cup (115g) golden syrup (or treacle)

2 cups (300g) plain (all-purpose) flour

1½ teaspoons bicarbonate of soda (baking soda)

2 tablespoons ground ginger

1 tablespoon ground cinnamon

⅔ cup (160ml) hot water

6 medium fresh figs (360g)

1 tablespoon caster (superfine) sugar, extra

toffee sauce

1 cup (220g) caster (superfine) sugar

½ cup (125ml) water

1¼ cups (310ml) thickened (heavy) cream

1 Have butter and eggs at room temperature.

2 Preheat oven to 180°C/350°F. Grease deep 22cm (9-inch) square cake pan; line base and sides with baking paper.

3 Peel pear; grate coarsely.

4 Beat butter and sugar in small bowl with electric mixer until light and fluffy. Beat in eggs, one at a time. Beat in syrup. Transfer mixture to large bowl; stir in sifted flour, soda and spices, pear and the hot water. Spread mixture into pan.

5 Bake cake about 1 hour. Stand cake in pan 10 minutes before turning, top-side up, onto wire rack.

6 Meanwhile, make toffee sauce.

7 Preheat grill (broiler). Cut figs in half; place, cut-side up, on oven tray. Sprinkle extra sugar over cut surface. Grill figs until browned lightly.

8 Top warm cake with figs; serve with warm toffee sauce, and cream or ice-cream, if you like.

TOFFEE SAUCE Combine sugar and the water in medium saucepan; stir over high heat, without boiling, until sugar dissolves. Bring to the boil; boil, uncovered, without stirring, until caramel in colour. Remove from heat. Carefully stir in cream (the mixture will spit and bubble). Stir over low heat until toffee pieces are melted and sauce is smooth.

prep + cook time 1½ hours
serves 12

note It is fine to use just the one 300ml carton of cream for this recipe.

rhubarb frangipane cake

250g (8 ounces) butter

3 eggs

1 bunch rhubarb (500g)

¼ cup (55g) caster (superfine) sugar

2 teaspoons vanilla extract

1 cup (220g) caster (superfine) sugar, extra

½ cup (120g) sour cream

1 cup (120g) ground almonds

1 cup (150g) self-raising flour

½ cup (75g) plain (all-purpose) flour

frangipane

60g (2 ounces) butter

1 egg

⅓ cup (75g) caster (superfine) sugar

1 cup (120g) ground almonds

2 tablespoons brandy

1 Have butter and eggs at room temperature.

2 Preheat oven to 180°C/350°F. Grease deep 22cm (9-inch) square cake pan; line base and sides with baking paper.

3 Trim rhubarb; cut into 12cm (5-inch) lengths. Cut thick stems in half lengthways so stems are about the same thickness to help them cook evenly. Toss rhubarb with sugar in shallow baking dish. Roast rhubarb, uncovered, about 20 minutes or until tender. Drain rhubarb; reserve syrup in dish. Cool.

4 Make frangipane.

5 Beat butter, extract and extra sugar in small bowl with electric mixer until light and fluffy. Beat in eggs, one at a time, then beat in sour cream. Transfer mixture to large bowl; stir in ground almonds and sifted flours. Spread mixture into pan. Spread frangipane over cake batter, top with rhubarb.

6 Bake cake about 1 hour. Stand cake in pan 10 minutes before turning, top-side up, onto wire rack. Brush with reserved rhubarb syrup.

7 Serve cake warm with cream or ice-cream, if you like.

FRANGIPANE Beat butter, egg and sugar in small bowl with electric mixer until creamy. Stir in ground almonds and brandy.

prep + cook time 2 hours (+ cooling) **serves** 15

cooking techniques

To chop dried apricots, use a pair of scissors. This is quicker and easier than using a knife. Wash and dry the scissors when they become sticky.

To grease a bundt pan, use a pastry brush to thickly coat the pan with soft butter. Sprinkle the pan with a little flour then tap out excess flour.

To extract the pulp and seeds from a pomegranate, cut it in half and hold it over a bowl. Hit it sharply with a wooden spoon – the seeds and pulp should fall out – if they don't, dig them out with a teaspoon.

To juice a pomegranate, cut it in half crossways and use a citrus juicer; strain the juice into a jug.

To hull a strawberry The hull, or calyx, is the green leafy top. Use a small, sharp knife to cut around the leafy top and into the pale flesh underneath, and discard. Wash and drain the strawberries before using.

To use a candy thermometer put it in a small saucepan of cold water, bring it to the boil. When the syrup begins to boil, put the thermometer into the syrup. Leave it in the syrup until the temperature required is reached, then return it to the pan of boiling water; turn the heat off, cool.

To make caramel (1), stir sugar and the water over high heat, without boiling, until the sugar dissolves. Use a pastry brush dipped in water to brush any sugar grains from the side of the pan back into the pan.

To make caramel (2), once the sugar has come to the boil, stop stirring and boil the mixture until the bubbles and large and thick and the colour is a golden amber (or until the required temperature is reached on a digital or candy thermometer).

o seed a vanilla pod, cut in half lengthwise with a harp knife. Hold the pod nd scrape the seeds out ith a spoon.

Zesting citrus fruit A zester has very small, and very sharp, holes that cut the rind (the outermost layer of the fruit) into thin ribbons but leaves the bitter white pith behind.

To grate a lime, use the small holes on a grater, ensuring only the rind is grated, and not the bitter white pith underneath. Rasp graters (thin metal graters), such as a Microplane grater, can also be used.

To toast coconut, stir in a dry frying pan over low heat until it turns a golden brown; as soon as it browns, remove it from the pan to stop it from overbrowning or burning.

o toast pistachios, stir e shelled nuts in a dry ying pan over low heat til they start to brown d become fragrant; as on they brown, remove om the pan to stop em from burning.

To separate an egg, set out two bowls. Crack the egg, and use your thumbs to gently pry the shell apart. Let the yolk settle in the lower half of the shell. Gently transfer the yolk back and forth between the shell halves, letting as much white as possible drip into the bowl. Be careful not to break the yolk. Place the yolk in a separate bowl.

To make simple chocolate curls, use a vegetable peeler and have a large bar of chocolate at room temperature. Drag the peeler down the length of the chocolate along the side to make small curls.

To melt chocolate, place roughly chopped chocolate into a heatproof bowl over a pan of barely simmering water. The water mustn't touch the base of the bowl. Stir chocolate until smooth, remove from the pan as soon as it's melted.

glossary

ALLSPICE also known as pimento or jamaican pepper; available whole or ground. Tastes like a blend of cinnamon, clove and nutmeg.

ALMOND flat, pointy-ended nut with pitted brown shell enclosing a creamy white kernel that is covered by a brown skin.
blanched whole nuts with brown skins removed.
flaked paper-thin almond slices.
meal also known as ground almonds; powdered to a flour-like texture and used in baking or as a thickening agent.
paste ground almonds, sugar and water cooked together until smooth. (Marzipan is almond paste to which more sugar has been added. It is more pliable, easier to roll, and is used for moulding and decorating.)

BAKING PAPER (parchment paper or baking parchment) a silicone-coated paper primarily used for lining baking pans and trays so cakes and biscuits won't stick, making removal easy.

BAKING POWDER a raising agent consisting of two parts cream of tartar to one part bicarbonate of soda.

BICARBONATE OF SODA also known as baking or carb soda; used as a leavening agent in baking.

BISCUITS also known as cookies.
granita made from flour, sugar, oil, wheat meal, butter, wheat flakes, golden syrup, egg and malt.
shortbread a pale golden, crumbly, buttery-tasting cookie made with just three ingredients: butter, sugar and flour (generally one part sugar, two parts butter, and three parts flour).

BLUEBERRIES a dark navy-blue to blue-black coloured round berry covered in a fine white powder or 'bloom'. Are small and sturdy, but are quite perishable, so keep them refrigerated and use as soon as possible.

BUTTER use salted or unsalted (sweet) butter; 125g is equal to one stick (4oz) of butter. *Unsalted butter* simply has no added salt. Is mainly used in baking; if the recipe calls for unsalted butter, then it should be used.

BUTTERMILK originally the term given to the slightly sour liquid left after butter was churned from cream, today it is commercially made similarly to yogurt. Sold alongside all fresh milk products in supermarkets; despite the implication of its name, it is low in fat.

CHEESE
cream cheese commonly known as Philadelphia or Philly, a soft cow's-milk cheese. Sold at supermarkets in bulk and packaged. Also available as spreadable light cream cheese, a blend of cottage and cream cheeses.
mascarpone a buttery-rich, cream-like cheese made from cow's milk. Ivory-coloured, soft and delicate, it has a sweet, slightly tangy, taste and a fat content of around 75%.
ricotta soft, white, cow's-milk cheese; roughly translates as 'cooked again'. It's made from whey, a by-product of other cheese making, to which fresh milk and acid are added. Ricotta is a sweet, moist cheese with a slightly grainy texture.

CHESTNUT PUREE found in some delicatessens and specialist food stores.

CHOCOLATE
dark eating also known as semi-sweet or luxury chocolate; made of a high percentage of cocoa liquor and cocoa butter, and a little added sugar.
milk most popular eating chocolate, mild and very sweet; similar in make-up to dark with the difference being the addition of milk solids.
white contains no cocoa solids but derives its sweet flavour from cocoa butter. Very sensitive to heat so watch carefully if melting.
chocolate-coated honeycomb bar a honeycomb confectionery that is covered in milk chocolate.
chocolate-hazelnut spread we use Nutella. Originally developed when chocolate was in short supply during World War 2, so hazelnuts were added to the chocolate supply.

CINNAMON SUGAR combination of ground cinnamon and caster sugar. To make your own: combine ½ cup caster sugar with 1 teaspoon cinnamon.

CLOVES dried flower buds of a tropical tree; can be used whole or in ground form. Has a distinctively pungent and 'spicy' scent and flavour.

COCOA POWDER also known as cocoa; dried, unsweetened, roasted and ground cocoa beans (cacao seeds). *Dutch cocoa* is treated with an alkali to neutralise its acids. It has a reddish-brown colour, a mild flavour and is easy to dissolve in liquids.

CORNFLOUR (cornstarch) used as a thickening agent. Available as 100% maize (corn) and wheaten cornflour.

CREAM we use fresh cream, also known as pouring cream and pure cream, unless otherwise stated. It has no additives, unlike commercially thickened cream, and has a minimum fat content of 35%.
double (thick) very rich, with a minimum fat content of 48%, it withstands boiling, and whips and freezes well.
sour a thick cultured soured cream. Minimum fat content 35%.
thickened (heavy) a whipping cream containing a thickener. Minimum fat content 35%.

COCONUT
desiccated dried, unsweetened, finely shredded coconut.
essence produced from coconut flavouring, oil and alcohol.
flaked dried, flaked coconut flesh.
shredded strips of dried coconut.

CREAM OF TARTAR acid ingredient in baking powder; keeps frostings creamy and improves volume when beating egg whites. Helps prevent sugar from crystallising when added to confectionery mixtures.

CUSTARD POWDER instant mixture used to make pouring custard; it is similar to North American instant pudding mixes.

FLOUR
plain an all-purpose flour made from wheat.
self-raising (rising) plain flour sifted with baking powder in the proportion of 1 cup flour to 2 teaspoons baking powder. Also called self-rising flour.

FOOD COLOURING dyes used to change the colour of foods. These dyes can be eaten and do not change the taste to a noticeable extent.

GELATINE a thickening agent. Available in sheet form, known as leaf gelatine or as a powder. Three teaspoons of powdered gelatine (8g or one sachet) is roughly equivalent to four gelatine leaves.

GINGER, GROUND also known as powdered ginger; used as a flavouring in cakes, pies and puddings but cannot be substituted for fresh ginger.

GLUCOSE SYRUP also known as liquid glucose; made from wheat starch. Used in jam and confectionery making. Available at health-food stores and supermarkets.

GOLDEN SYRUP a by-product of refined sugarcane; pure maple syrup or honey can be substituted.

GRENADINE SYRUP an extremely sweet non-alcoholic syrup, traditionally made from pomegranates. It is used as an ingredient in cocktails, both for its flavour and to give a reddish/pink tinge to mixed drinks. These days it can be made with other fruits, including cherries and blackberries.

HAZELNUTS also known as filberts; plump, grape-sized, rich, sweet nut.
meal known as ground hazelnuts.

JAM also known as preserve or conserve; most often made from fruit.

KAFFIR LIME LEAVES also known as bai magrood, sold fresh, dried or frozen; looks like two glossy dark green leaves joined end to end, forming a rounded hourglass shape. Dried leaves are less potent, so double the number called for in a recipe if you substitute them for fresh leaves. A strip of fresh lime peel may be substituted for each kaffir lime leaf.

LEMON GRASS a tall, clumping, lemon-smelling and -tasting, sharp-edged grass; the white lower part of the stem is chopped and used in cooking. Bruise the lower white bulb with the flat side of a heavy knife to release the flavour and aroma.

LIQUEURS
coffee liqueur we use Kahlúa or Tia Maria in our recipes, but you can use your favourite brand.
cointreau citrus-flavoured liqueur. Its subtle taste is due to the blend of fragrant peels from oranges.
framboise raspberry-flavoured liqueur; Creme de Framboises is sweeter.
frangelico a traditional hazelnut liqueur.
hazelnut we use Frangelico but you can use your favourite brand.
kirsch cherry-flavoured liqueur.
orange-flavoured we use Grand Marnier, which is based on cognac-brandy. Use your favourite brand.

MARZIPAN see almond paste.

MILO brand name of a sweetened chocolate malted milk drink base.

MINT a herb that includes many varieties including spearmint, common mint and peppermint. Spearmint has long, smooth leaves, and is the one that greengrocers sell, while common mint, with rounded, pebbly leaves, is the one that most people grow. Spearmint has the stronger flavour.

MIXED SPICE a blend of ground spices usually consisting of cinnamon, allspice and nutmeg.

MUSCAT a sweet, fruity dessert wine, made from the grape of the same name. Is almost caramel in colour.

MUSCATELS, DRIED made by drying large muscatel grapes (grown almost exclusively around Malaga in Spain). They are partially dried in the sun and drying is completed indoors; they are left on the stalk and pressed flat for sale. Muscatel is a sweet wine made from the grapes.

MUSLIN a loosely-woven cotton fabric used to separate liquid from solids. May also be used to wrap dried herbs before adding to a dish and used to infuse flavour into sauces.

NASHI a member of the pear family but resembling an apple with its pale-yellow-green, tennis-ball-sized appearance; more commonly known as the Asian pear. Is different from other pears in that it is crisp and juicy.

NECTAR is a form of fruit juice that tends to be very sweet and rich. It is made by pressing the fruit concerned, and often includes some of the pulp, making it very thick.

NOUGAT a confectionery made from honey, nuts and egg whites. The nougat we are most familiar with is the chewy white confectionery studded with nuts, however, it can be either soft and chewy or crunchy.

NUTMEG dried nut of an evergreen tree native to Indonesia; it is available in ground form or you can grate your own with a fine grater.

NUTS
to roast nuts, spread shelled nuts in a single layer on an oven tray; roast in a 180°C/350°F oven for eight to 10 minutes, stirring occasionally, until golden and fragrant. They burn easily, so watch carefully.
to toast nuts, place shelled nuts in a single layer in a small dry frying pan; stir, over low heat, until fragrant and just changed in colour. They burn easily, so watch carefully.

ORANGE FLOWER WATER is a concentrated flavouring made from orange blossoms. Available from Middle-Eastern food stores and some delicatessens. Cannot be substituted with citrus flavourings, as the taste is completely different.

PASSIONFRUIT (granadilla) a small tropical fruit, native to Brazil, has a tough outer skin that surrounds edible black, sweet-sour, seeds.

PASTRY
fillo is unique in that no margarine or fat is added to the dough. The dough, which is very elastic in texture, is not rolled like other pastries, but stretched to the desired thickness. This gives it its unique, delicate, tissue-thin sheets. It is best brushed with margarine or butter before baking.
puff a crisp, light pastry; layers of dough and margarine are folded and rolled many times making many layers. When baked, it becomes a high, crisp, flaky pastry. Sheets of frozen puff pastry are available from supermarkets.

Butter puff pastry uses butter for the shortening, whereas other puff pastry uses a commercially made blend of vegetable and animal fats.

shortcrust a tender, crunchy, melt-in-the-mouth buttery pastry. Once baked it is a light, crumbly, easily broken short pastry. Packaged sheets of shortcrust pastry are available from supermarkets. Also comes as sweet or savoury varieties.

PEACHES come in yellow and white varieties, both of which can be either clingstone or freestone, defined by whether the flesh separates cleanly from the stone. White peaches are fragile, so can't be used for lengthy cooking periods, such as pies.

PECANS native to the United States and now grown locally; is a golden-brown, buttery and rich-tasting nut.

PEANUT BRITTLE peanuts coated in a hard toffee coating; available from confectionery stores and most major supermarkets.

PRUNES commercially or sun-dried plums; store in the fridge.

PURE MAPLE SYRUP a thin syrup distilled from the sap of the maple tree. Maple-flavoured syrup or pancake syrup is not an adequate substitute for the real thing.

RAISINS dried sweet grapes.

RASPBERRIES known as the 'king of the berries'; about 1.5-2cm long, cylinder-shaped, with a deep red colouring and a sweet flavour. Also available black or yellow in colour. Are actually a collection of tiny fruits, each with its own seed covered in red skin and flesh, which form a cluster around a small stem. When harvested, the cluster comes away from the stem leaving the centre hollow. Are fragile and spoil rapidly, so check for mildew when buying. Also available frozen.

RHUBARB has thick, celery-like stalks that can reach up to 60cm in length; the stalks are the only edible portion of the plant – the leaves contain a toxic substance. Though rhubarb is generally eaten as a fruit, it is actually a vegetable.

ROSE PETAL JAM made from organic rose petals simmered in sugar, water and lemon juice. From Middle-Eastern stores.

ROSEWATER distilled from rose petals, and used in the Middle East, North Africa, and India to flavour desserts. Don't confuse this with rose essence, which is more concentrated.

RUBY GRAPEFRUIT is the pink version of grapefruit. Eat on its own or in fruit salads, salads, sorbets and granitas.

RUM, UNDERPROOF the term 'proof' dates back to the days when buyers wanted to be sure they weren't getting watered down liqueur, so they mixed equal amounts of rum and gunpowder and set it alight – if it burned it was 'proof' that the correct amount of alcohol was here, if it didn't it was underproof. The term now refers to an alcohol content of 50% by volume (abv) or 100 proof. Underproof means the rum is less than 50% abv, and overproof means the rum is over 50% abv.

SAFFRON THREADS available in strands or ground form; imparts a yellow-orange colour to food once infused. Quality varies greatly; the best is the most expensive spice in the world. Should be stored in the freezer.

SORBET a frozen dessert made with fruit juice or another flavouring, a sweetener (usually sugar), and beaten egg whites, which prevent the formation of large ice crystals.

SULTANAS dried grapes, also known as golden raisins.

SUGAR
brown a soft, fine sugar retaining molasses. *Dark brown* is a moist, dark brown sugar with a rich distinctive flavour coming from molasses syrup.
caster also known as superfine or finely granulated table sugar.
demerara golden colour with a subtle molasses flavour. The fine syrup coating on the crystal, together with its coarseness, gives a good colour to the crust of baking.

icing also known as confectioners' sugar or powdered sugar; granulated sugar crushed together with a small amount of added cornflour.
raw natural brown granulated sugar.
white a coarse, granulated table sugar, also known as crystal sugar.

SWEET DESSERT WINE also known as fortified wines. Common fortified wines include sherry, port, vermouth, and marsala.

SWEETENED CONDENSED MILK a canned milk product; 60% of the water is removed and the remaining milk is then sweetened with sugar.

TREACLE a thick, dark syrup not unlike molasses; is a by-product of sugar refining. Treacle can be substituted with golden syrup.

TURKISH DELIGHT an extremely popular Middle-Eastern sweet. Its Turkish name is rahat lokum – meaning 'rest' for the throat. A mixture of syrup and cornflour is boiled with either honey or fruit juice. Most often flavoured with rosewater or peppermint. Once set, the mixture is rolled in icing sugar. Turkish delight is available commercially in confectionery shops and most major supermarkets.

VANILLA
bean dried long, thin pod from a tropical orchid grown in Central and South America and Tahiti; the tiny black seeds impart a luscious vanilla flavour in baking and desserts.
extract made by extracting the flavour from the vanilla bean pods, which are soaked in alcohol to capture the authentic flavour.
paste made from vanilla pods and contains real seeds. It is highly concentrated and 1 teaspoon replaces a whole vanilla pod without mess or fuss as you neither have to split or scrape the pod. It is found in the baking aisle of many supermarkets.

YOGURT, GREEK full-cream yogurt, often made from sheep milk; its thick, smooth consistency, almost like whipped cream, is attained by draining off the milk liquids.

index

Published in 2012 by ACP Books, Sydney
ACP Books are published by ACP Magazines Limited,
a division of Nine Entertainment Co.

ACP BOOKS

Publishing Director, ACP Magazines Gerry Reynolds
Publisher Sally Wright
Editor-in-chief Susan Tomnay
Creative director & designer Hieu Chi Nguyen
Art director Hannah Blackmore
Senior editor Wendy Bryant
Food director Pamela Clark
Food editor Rebecca Squadrito
Sales & rights director Brian Cearnes
Special sales manager Simone Aquilina
Acting marketing manager Sonia Scali
Marketing assistant Madeleine Jelfs
Senior business analyst Rebecca Varela
Operations manager David Scotto
Circulation manager Sarah Lloyd
Circulation analyst Nicole Pearson
Published by ACP Books, a division of
ACP Magazines Ltd, 54 Park St, Sydney;
GPO Box 4088, Sydney, NSW 2001.
phone (02) 9282 8618; fax (02) 9267 9438.

acpbooks@acpmagazines.com.au;
www.acpbooks.com.au

Printed by Toppan Printing Co, China.

Australia Distributed by Network Services,
phone +61 2 9282 8777; fax +61 2 9264 3278;
networkweb@networkservicescompany.com.au
New Zealand Distributed by Netlink Distribution Company,
phone (64 9) 366 9966; ask@ndc.co.nz
South Africa Distributed by PSD Promotions,
phone (27 11) 392 6065/6/7; fax (27 11) 392 6079/80;
orders@psdprom.co.za

Title: Show-stopper desserts / food director, Pamela Clark.
ISBN: 9-781-74245-240-1 (pbk.)
Notes: Includes index.
Subjects: Desserts.
Other Authors/Contributors: Clark, Pamela.
Dewey Number: 641.86

© ACP Magazines Ltd 2012
ABN 18 053 273 546
Recipe development Lucy Nunes; Alexandra Elliott; Kerrie Carr
Nutritional information Rebecca Squadrito

Photographer Ian Wallace
Stylist Louise Pickford
Food preparation Adam Cremona
Cover Honey and saffron pears, page 42

The publishers would like to thank the following
for props used in photography:
Camargue, Parterre, Redelman Fabrics, Seletti,
Villeroy & Boch, WWRD, Liley & Liley

To order books
phone 136 116 (within Australia) or
order online at www.acpbooks.com.au
Send recipe enquiries to:
recipeenquiries@acpmagazines.com.au

First published in 2012

ACP Books are published by ACP Magazines Limited,

a division of Nine Entertainment Co.

54 Park St, Sydney

GPO Box 4088, Sydney, NSW 2001.

phone (02) 9282 8618; fax (02) 9267 9438

acpbooks@acpmagazines.com.au; www.acpbooks.com.au

ACP BOOKS

Publishing Director, ACP Magazines - Gerry Reynolds

Publisher - Sally Wright

Editor-in-Chief - Susan Tomnay

Creative Director - Hieu Chi Nguyen

Food Director - Pamela Clark

Published and Distributed in the United Kingdom by Octopus Publishing Group

Endeavour House

189 Shaftesbury Avenue

London WC2H 8JY

United Kingdom

phone (+44)(0)207 632 5400; fax (+44)(0)207 632 5405

info@octopus-publishing.co.uk;

www.octopusbooks.co.uk

Printed by Toppan Printing Co., China

International foreign language rights, Brian Cearnes, ACP Books bcearnes@acpmagazines.com.au

A catalogue record for this book is available from the British Library.

ISBN 978-1-907428-49-4

© ACP Magazines Ltd 2012

ABN 18 053 273 546